First Nation Stories Anthology

Charlie Venne

Copyright © 2023 by Charlie Venne

All rights reserved.

No portion of this book may be reproduced in any form without written permission from the publisher or author, except as permitted by USA copyright law.

This story is dedicated to the many Missing and Murdered Indigenous Women and Girls (MMIWG).

There has been a devastating epidemic of lost sisters, mothers, aunties, and grandmothers. At the time of this story's writing 2000-2001, there was no such inquiry of our missing Indigenous women. Today there are action plans, websites, social media pages, video channels and so much more in the public eye.

Who was there when our sisters went missing long ago?

One of my first my inspirations was my late grandfather – nimosōm (Cree). As a boy growing up, he used to tell me all kinds of stories and legends. The stories he told would bring my imagination to life (1980s).

My second inspiration is my mother. She used to love reading my hand-written stories and would try to encourage me to enter story-writing contests on various magazines (1990s).

My most recent inspiration is my beautiful wife, Jenny. I told her about my dreams and told me to go for it and see what happens. Here I am, and I am going to see what happens.

Contents

1. RedDress — 1
2. The Return of the Wihtikō — 20
3. Into the Life's Circle — 44
4. Kipochh the Wanderer — 49
5. Kipochh Saves The Sun (According To Him) — 52
6. Kipoch Mounts a Ride — 56
7. Moon Rising — 58
8. Chris and Amanda — 65
9. Joe and the Stranger — 70
10. Maci-Pimithākan – UFO — 73
11. The Eagle Flies into the Past — 77
12. Sōniyāw Reserve — 80

About the Author — 93

About The Publisher — 95

More From Eaglespeaker Publishing — 97

Chapter One

RedDress

Circa, 1910 boreal area of central Saskatchewan

Two young explorers are travelling in a canoe through a vast river system, seeking adventure. They've been travelling for many weeks and have not run into any hostile "Indians" as they expected. In fact, the trip had been getting quite tedious and predictable.

Several hours into their trip, they noticed commotion from a tiny community, more of a large camp site. The boys slowly paddle on the shore and sneak towards the camp. They see a young lady going to the landing with what appears to be a birch bark basket, likely to haul water.

The young travelers whisper to themselves and one asks the other, "What should we do?" The other young man grins and nods his head, as his eyes lustfully examine the young Native woman scooping up water.

Circa, 2000 boreal area of central Saskatchewan.

Kristina trots along the road on her way home from school. She is 16 years of age and ready to enjoy the summer. It was the last day of school, and she couldn't wait to have some fun.

She wonders how much fun she could have since she lives in such a small town. A northern community does not exactly have all the modern amenities a southern city has, so she would have to be content. As she ponders her sad life, she crosses the road nonchalantly, when suddenly an old truck turns toward her and sideswipes her. She goes flying off the road and lands on her side, banging her head on the ground.

Next thing she knows, she is lying in a hospital bed and can't remember anything. *"awināna, kākī-pamihcikīt?"* she asks.

"Excuse me?" says the doctor, *"I'm afraid I don't understand Cree."* he apologizes.

"Neither do I," says Kristina groggily, *"I just asked who was driving, do you know?"*

The doctor shakes his head, *"I could've sworn you just spoke Cree to me, but to answer your question, we don't know who it was. However, from what I've heard, the truck that hit you had been speeding and swerving, so there's a good chance it may have been a drunk driver."* explains the doctor, *"How are you feeling? You took quite a bump."*

"My head is killing me; did I break anything?"

"I don't think so, but we have to keep you in for a while, we need to run some tests to make sure you'll be alright."

"Fine, I feel a little woozy, but I think I'll be okay."

Days later, Kristina gets out of the hospital and goes home to a pair of worried parents. *"How are you feeling baby? Can I get you something?"* asks her mother gently.

"No thanks, I think I'll just go to bed; my head still hurts a little."

"Okay, you go on to bed, and in the morning, I'll cook you a giant breakfast."

"Thanks mom, good night"

"Good night baby! Are you sure you don't need anything?"

"No, I'll be fine, good night." Kristina crawls into bed and falls asleep right away. On the windowsill, a factory-made dreamcatcher slightly twirls and gently drops on the floor. Kristina stirs but goes right back to sleep.

In a dream, Kristina is holding a birch bark basket, standing at the landing of a beautiful river, much like the one close to her school but with no roads or houses on the side. She is wearing a buck skin dress and none of her usual make-up. She stares at the river in awe because it is so clear and sparkling; she wonders who might have cleaned up the usually dirty and murky river. She dips her basket in to gather up some water and takes a sip. At the corner of her eye, she sees a couple of pale men staring at her from the shoreline of the river. The men are in a canoe loaded with supplies covered in a blanket. She gets ready to run, but instead, her curiosity takes over. One of the young men uncovers the supplies to reveal a shiny satin red dress. Kristina's eyes widen in delight. She has heard of white men offering gifts to her people, but she never thought it would happen to her. What she did not hear, was that the white men always wanted something in return. As she reached out for the dress, the young man grabs her and covers her mouth. Kristina kicks and screams in shear horror and confusion.

Suddenly, Kristina wakes up in a cold sweat with tears coming down her eyes. She had such a bad dream she found herself sobbing. Kristina did not have any misgivings for non-native people and found them quite polite and respectful when she talked to them. However, the feeling she was feeling now was not that of respect or admiration, but of fear and distrust. She ponders her feelings for a while and goes back to sleep after concluding her paranoia about non-native people was silly.

The next day, Kristina wanders around the community wondering what to do with her time. She runs into one of her old friends: Andrew.

Andrew is a tall brainy type of person who is also deeply into Indian politics and political correctness. "Hello! Kristina, how's the hit and run victim doing?" he asks.

"Quite well Mr. Indigenous man, how are you?" Kristina responds.

"Cut that out, you know I don't like the racially insensitive word, 'Indian,' I prefer the correct term. Not the term governs to us by Euro-Canadians who ripped huge amounts of land out from under our feet, and leaving us with specks of dirt..."

"Okay, okay, I get the picture, I just asked how you were doing, I didn't want a lecture on Indian, I mean 'Indigenous' studies." Kristina says, rolling up her eyes.

"I'm sorry Kristina, but I just get so mad when I think of the past dealings with the Canadian government. I only wish it was me who negotiated the treaties for the First people." Andrew apologizes, "In fact, I'm on my way to the band office to give them advice on how to deal with Indian Affairs, want to join me?"

"No thanks, I'm sure you'll have enough to say for the both of us." Kristina says as she walks away.

It was not that long after she met with Andrew that Kristina ran into an old medicine man who everybody avoids. She was no different; she decided to walk around him to avoid him. Usually, it is an easy task because the shaman usually pays her no attention. However, this time, the medicine man looks up at Kristina and stares at her as if fearful of something, he yells out "Red dress is trying to talk to you, listen to her"

Kristina freaks out and wonders what the old man could be talking about. "Alright!" Kristina said, "I'll listen to her." she adds as she hurriedly walks away as fast as she could. It was such a surprise that the old man talked to her that she did not even think about what he meant.

Kristina strolls along and remains confused about the recent events that have happened. What did the dream mean? What was the old man talking about? She thought of going to Andrew for some answers, but she wasn't willing to put herself into his crazy world. He gets too darn political and would probably go on and on about the treaties and how our ancestors were screwed. No, she did not want to go through that. Then she had an idea, she would ask her grandma. Yeah! Granny seems to know everything. Upon her decision, she realized that she was near the river where she saw herself in her dream.

Her feelings border on surreal. She could not describe what she felt but she felt some type of connection with the river. She has been there many times, but she's never felt this way before. She decides to check out the shoreline and tries to put herself in her dream. She carefully walks along the shoreline, and then at the corner of her eye, she sees a hazy figure. Kristina's heart beats a mile a minute as she slowly looks up at the figure. There she is a young woman wearing a red dress. Her face looks pleasant, as she is smiling. The dress looks wrinkly and frumpy, but the girl seems pleased with it. "Hi!" Kristina says, "What's your name?" she asks.

The girl just smiles, but her smile slowly turns to a sad frown. She looks down and looks back up as her face distinctly becomes older before Kristina's eyes. Kristina blinks her eyes and tries to focus. The girl then screams out "wīcihin! wīcihin! nisāminik awa mōniyāw! – Help me! Help me! This white man is touching me" as she begins to struggle with an unseen assailant.

"I don't understand Cree!" Kristina screams, "What's happening to you?"

" wīcihin! kāwitha mosci kinawāpamin! – Help me! Don't just look at me!" the girl pleads as her face now appears to slowly rot.

Kristina goes running to the girl, and just before she gets to her, the girl completely disappears. "What, where are you?" Kristina says, "Where are you, what's happening?" Kristina says.

Girl in a Dream

The girl does not reappear. Kristina can only guess what might have happened. She was very confused and frightened with what just happened to her. What did she just see? She decides to follow her first instinct, ask somebody who might know: her grandma. Her grandmother was very colonized and a devout Christian, but she might be her only hope to figure out her mysterious situation.

Kristina sits down on her grandma's couch as she hums along an old country tune and wonders how to start her request off. She would occasionally look to her grandma to see if she were suspicious of anything. "Hi kohkom, how have you been?"

"pīyakwan, kīthamāka? – I have been the same, what about you?" her grandma asks.

"I've been good," Kristina responds, "I've never been better" she adds.

"I can tell," her grandma said," you usually don't even respond to Cree words."

"What Cree words?" Kristina says.

"Hmmm! What did you come to see me for?"

"Can't I visit my own grandma once in a while?"

"I guess so, since I haven't seen you in over a month."

"Okay, I won't lie to you kohkom, I am really freaked out. I've been having dreams of a Native girl wearing a red dress, and I'm her; I can feel what she is going through. I might be possessed by her spirit, and nobody is going to understand. I need your help."

"God gives help when it is needed, but not when it has to do with stupid old Indian beliefs. When are you and your generation going to understand, there is no spiritual things happening. Only shameful Indians believe that stuff. Jesus will help us; he is the savior, not some spiritual Indian medicine. We were freed from that superstition. We only need God now."

"Please kohkom, this is different, I feel horrible beings having their way with something they shouldn't, and I want them to stop." Kristina pleads.

"You know that spiritual stuff Indians mess with nowadays, that's bad medicine. The Bible released us from that Evil stupidity; I don't know why you youngsters pay attention to it."

"Kohkom, I don't care about that stuff, I just want to understand what's happening to me."

"I'm not sure, but whatever it is, it's probably no good. I want you out of my blessed house. I really don't want an Indian spiritual atheist in my house. Please leave now" her grandma says, "And by the way, I hope God forgives you for your sins."

"But I haven't sinned, I think. I need your help to find out what's happening to me. A girl from the past is haunting me. I think she needs my help with something, but I don't know what." Kristina explains.

"A girl from the past?" her grandma says, as she squints her eyes.

"Yes, I don't know why, but she's been in my head lately and I think she's trying to tell me something." At that moment, Kristina remembers what the Medicine man said to her. Something about listening to Red Dress, could that be her name? "Kohkom, did you ever hear the name 'Red Dress?'"

Her grandmother slowly turns toward her, "Red Dress?" her grandma says somberly, "There is an old story about a spirit called Red Dress, but I haven't heard it in a long time. Who told you about it?"

"Nobody, I just remember the old Medicine man mention the name and told me to listen to Red Dress. I don't know what he meant, but in my dream, the Indian girl I see is wearing a red dress." Kristina grits her teeth as she anticipates an outburst from her grandma.

"Hmmm! The old Medicine man, eh? John was always one to scare children, but what's he trying to do now? Offer spiritual help? Ha! The idiot wouldn't know a peace pipe if he was hit with one." her grandma crows,

"I'll tell you what, I'll tell the whole story about Red Dress and you can draw your own conclusions, okay?"

"Okay, tell me."

RED Dress

Her grandmother starts off thoughtfully and with surprising care:

Red Dress was a young lady who everybody thought was the most beautiful girl in the world, and it was felt that she belonged someplace better. She was kind, pretty, and got along with anybody, it didn't matter who. Her problem was that she was a very curious girl; she always had to know what was going on or how things worked. One day, a pair of white explorers came by the community in their canoe. Red Dress had been down by the river at the time to haul water for her mother. That was the last time Red Dress was ever seen. It was later agreed that she joined the explorers on their journey. Because of her extreme propensity to satisfy her curiosity, nobody argued otherwise. It was just accepted as true. The part about the Red Dress spirit sightings were made up by Indians who wouldn't accept the real story and instead, came up with their own to express their anger. More than likely, it was a ploy to hold on to dumb Indian beliefs, and to reject Jesus Christ as our savior.

Kristina questions the validity of the story. Why was the girls' name 'Red Dress' when there were no red Indian dresses at the time she was around, and why do her dreams contradict the story, especially about Red Dress joining the explorers? The story makes it sound like Red Dress lives happily ever after, but in her dream, the explorers are doing something inappropriate to her, like what seems like raping her. What did happen to Red Dress?

If she did not go back home, then where did she go? Kristina asks these questions to her grandmother.

"It's only a story Kristina!" her grandmother asserts, "The dreams you're having are probably nothing, but fantasies brought on by raging hormones."

"What do you mean, raging hormones?" asks an even more confused Kristina.

"Never mind, but it is only dreams, they don't mean anything. I'm sure you'll be just fine, just don't go to that medicine man. He'll really mix things up for you."

"Okay, thanks for your help." Kristina says, "even if you didn't help me." she whispers.

That night, Kristina was up in her room browsing the Internet. She decides she would do some research on her own, research on past explorations in Canada. She found the usual stuff about John Cabot and Samuel Hearne, but nothing on two young men going on their own. Obviously, there would be little hope in finding records of independent travels made by early Canadians, but she wants to find some type of link. After many hours of searching, Kristina gave up and went to bed. She would have to figure out something tomorrow.

In her dream, Kristina again finds herself at the river. This time however, she is herself. She walks along the river and hears some commotion further along. She slowly creeps up to see what's happening. At the distance, she sees a young man struggling with a young lady on the grassy shore of the river. She starts toward them until she sees another young man looking down at them. She quickly ducks down to avoid being seen and watches them. She should help her, she thinks to herself, and then realizes that what she is seeing happened in the past and cannot do anything about it. She stands up and walks over to them. Not fearing their detection, she goes right up to the young man watching and looks down at the struggle. She feels a knot in her stomach as she realizes the young lady has stopped struggling and is being raped. The young man gets off her and tells his partner that it's his turn. The other man gets down and notices the girl is lying very still with her eyes closed, "What's wrong with her William?" he cries, "She's not moving at all."

William gets on one knee to check her out, "Oh my God!" he says, "I think she's dead, I think I killed her."

"Why did you squeeze her neck so hard? You should have been more careful."

"I thought she stopped struggling because she liked it," William reasons, and then realizes, "My God! I just had sex with a corpse; I'm going to burn in Hell!"

"Holy cow! What do we do? The Indians are going to kill us if they find out."

"Wait a minute, they don't know we're here, we'll just leave her here and bugger off, they'll never know it was us."

"We can't just leave her here; we have to bury her or something."

The boys fetch their shovel and pick a spot, deep in the woods to bury her. After they finish, they hurry off into the unknown, never having to pay for their crimes, and leaving a disgruntled, molested spirit to lament her own death as she watches the boys paddle down the river.

Kristina looks tenderly at the spirit of Red Dress and starts to cry. She knew that nobody else besides her, knew what really happened. She only wishes she could help in some way, "Please tell me how I can help you?" she pleads, and as she says this, Red Dress quickly turns and looks at her.

John Red Bear

That morning, Kristina slowly gets up and examines her surroundings. She gets dressed up and goes downstairs to join her parents for breakfast. "Good morning!" her mother says cheerfully, "how did you sleep? Do you feel okay?"

"I feel fine mom," Kristina says," how are you feeling?"

"Great! Ah, why are dressed like that?" her mom says as she looks at Kristina's red dress, "Are you going out to a party?"

"Party?" Kristina asks, "Yes, I am going to a party." she says, reassuringly.

"Well, that's nice, whose party is it?"

"A friend's, you wouldn't know her."

"Okay then, finish eating your food before you go, okay?"

"Alright mom." It is not long before Kristina is out the door and off to her pretend party. She runs into her old pal, Andrew. "Hello Andrew, how are you this morning?"

"Just fine Kristina," Andrew responds, as he stands there waiting," well, what happened to your snappy greetings, I was looking forward to some sarcasm today, and I thought you might oblige." he continues.

"I am sorry Andrew, how was the band office conciliation?"

Andrew curiously looks down at Kristina's dress, then dismisses it "Not too well," Andrew said, "they told me that they didn't need my opinion until I was of voting age. Can you believe that rubbish? I guess they want to remain ignorant to real First Nations issues, I'm willing to bet that they don't even know the least bit of history of our ancestors."

"Exactly," Kristina responds, "I am willing to bet that they can't even speak our language or mend a birch bark canoe."

"Well neither do I, but that's not what I'm talking about, "Andrew says, "I was talking about the use of renewable natural resources. Don't you know we have berries, forests, and animals that can be harvested to improve the financial situation of our community?"

"Financial situation? I thought you were talking about Native tradition and its importance to future generations." Kristina says, "And do you mean to tell me that you can't even speak Cree? Or mend a birch bark canoe? I thought you were a real First Nations person, but your just an over ambitious hypocrite who thinks the world of himself just because he has an education!"

"Now, now, calm down Kristina, no need to get excited." Andrew assures, "I just feel that Indian Affairs is controlling us too much and I want it to stop that's all." Andrew adds, but then ponders Kristina's words for a while, "Speak Cree and mend canoes? What the hell are you talking about?" Asks Andrew, "Since when do you know how to do that?"

"I don't," Kristina says, "I just thought that's what you meant. I really have get going, see ya later." says Kristina as she hurriedly walks away.

Andrew stands there scratching his head, "Wow! Come to think of it, I do feel like a hypocrite."

Kristina is strolling along the road when suddenly a car pulls up beside her, "Do you know where the nearest gas station is?" a nasal voice said, "I'm running a little low on gas."

Kristina bends down to see who it is and notices that it is a non-native man wearing a baseball cap, "No! Get away from me!" Kristina screams," Help! Help! There's a white man trying to attack me." she screams again, as she attracts the attention of two Native teenagers hanging out at a playground.

The two guys go running up to Kristina and ask her what is wrong, and she tells them: "That white man was trying to pick me up."

The boys go sprinting up to the car and start yelling at the man, "Get the heck out of here you desperate sicko." said one of them. "And leave our girls along you white pervert." said the other.

"But I didn't do anything, I don't know what she's talking about." the man says.

Kristina, in her tears, realizes what just happened, "Wait a minute! I didn't mean it, I don't know what came over me, leave that man alone."

The boys look at Kristina, one of them says, "What! Leave him alone? You just said he tried to attack you."

"I'm sorry, it was a mistake, he didn't do anything." Kristina explains.

"I'm very sorry sir; the bitch is just crazy I guess." The boys go back to the playground and the man drives away without saying a word.

Kristina arrives at the river and sits down to try and get her head straight. She views the river much differently now and wonders if she'll ever look at it the same way again. As she is sitting on the grass, a shadow casts over her and its John the medicine man that everybody avoids. Kristina stands up "What do you want?" she demands.

"You know, an old white man used to come to this community," John started, "It was during the fifties before we could even drink in a bar." he continues, "He used to offer us rides in his truck, take us to town when we needed it or drop us off at a trap line if there was a road. What I used to like was when he would go to the bar for us and pick up some liqueur. Ha-Ha! We used to have such a great time in those days. He was quite the character. Then one day, while we were gathered for a feast, he got up and told us how sorry he was for what he had done and how he would never forgive himself. He did not say what it was, just that he was sorry. His face was filled with sorrow, and I could tell he really was sorry. After he left, many of the people dismissed what he had to say because of his generosity, but I knew what he meant. He was apologizing for something he should never be forgiven for." John continues, "Red Dress was my mother's younger sister, and they would wander around the river side whenever they had time to spare. Red Dress was not her real name; her real name was Sunrise because she was born on the first morning of summer. Sunrise was thought to have left with a pair of explorers, but my mother knew otherwise. However, nobody would listen to her. Everybody kept telling her to forget about it and accept the fact that she was out seeing the world she wanted to see.

Because nobody would listen to her, she would tell me the story, which is why I knew what the old man was talking about. Up until that time, even I disregarded my mother's stories as stubborn and foolish. My mother would tell me over and over again, 'never accept anything from the white man'. She didn't trust them or believe the so-called 'Good News' they carried with them. She continued to practice Native Spirituality and passed it along to me. Today, I am greatly outnumbered by the 'assimilated people.' I am the only one that can help you."

Kristina stands there wondering what to say, or even think. Could this be the only person who can help her? Andrew's help is out of the question, he'd probably lecture her on being a believer of the supernatural, unless it was financially beneficial. Kohkom would kill her if I mentioned another spirit, and my parents are only my parents. So, I guess that leaves her with one choice: "How can you help us?"

The Conclusion

John leads Kristina to his place. It is an old cabin by the river, not too far away is what looks like a sweat lodge. "We're going to go in that!" Kristina asks, "My Kohkom would kill me if she heard about it. She thinks all Native religion practices are evil and devilish, I can't go in there."

"This was the first church of our people." John responds, "Not the over-sized monstrosities that Christian followers go to. In the sweat lodge, there is no money involved, and no blood sacrifice of a sacred person."

"Of course not, we're much better than that, right?"

"No! It is not about being better, it is about following what truly belongs to you and not to another race of people who lack respect for you." retorts

John, "I have no ill feelings toward the intentions of their religion, the intentions are good, and the advice is priceless. However, the people who practice it are hypocrites, who, more often than not, break the rules of their own religion. It is very shameful what they do, to themselves, and to the Great Spirit."

"Don't you mean God?" Kristina says.

"They are one and the same, they are just named differently." explains John.

That afternoon, John and Kristina sit at the appropriate places in the lodge as they close their eyes and ask for guidance. In Kristina's mind, there are pieces of the past flashing before her eyes. She sees Sunrise standing beside the river. She turns toward her and starts to slowly float toward her. Kristina's stands there as she weeps for the spirit coming to her, she holds out her arms to embrace her. Suddenly, Sunrise stops at about ten feet from Kristina and just looks at her. She appears to lift her head and rise her arms in joy when all of a sudden; she floats right into Kristina, and she falls down.

Kristina had run out of the sweat lodge and crumples on the grass. John comes after her and places a blanket over her. "Are you okay?" John asks, "What happened?"

"I don't know." answers Kristina," I felt a cold breeze go over me during my vision."

"Your vision?" Says John, "What did you see?"

"I saw Sunrise. She seemed happy about something. Like she was able finally to do something, but I don't know what."

"What did she say?" "Nothing, her face said it all; she was happy about something."

The next day, Kristina set out for the river again. John was standing there looking at the water flowing. He was holding a roll of a newspaper. "What's that you're holding?"

"A newspaper," says John," it's got some interesting news, you want to hear it?"

"What does it say?" "It says, ' A one hundred and fifteen-year-old man died yesterday'"

"Wow, that old huh? That is interesting news."

"That's not the interesting part."

"What do you mean?"

"He left a personal note in his will that said 'A man like me doesn't deserve to live so long, when I finally do pass on, it will be with a heavy heart. I only hope I will be forgiven for the terrible thing I've done to an innocent life who only wanted to wear a red dress.' The family doesn't know what to make of the note, but they had it printed because he wanted it to be."

"Could it be the man who did it?"

"Could be, it says he passed on in the afternoon yesterday. I think about the time we were in the sweat lodge." John looks down on Kristina." I believe she was finally released to the next world. Where she could start at the place she left off, in the great circle of life."

...

Sunrise runs through the wide, open grassy meadow, feeling the warm breeze over her face and the beauty of the landscape pleasing her eyes. She feels that she may have been sleeping for too long, but now the earthly demise of the one who stole innocence, beauty, and pride from her is gone. Now nobody and nothing can prevent her from going forward.

Chapter Two

The Return of the Wihtikō

Jack Williams

It was twilight in the early spring when Jack Williams came back from another long walk from checking his traps. It was near the end of the trapping season, and he was dreading having to go back to the city. He thought of how lucky the Natives were on the reserve as his lodge was near the Sōniyāw Reserve. They get to stay here year-round with their families, jobs, and hobbies. Everything seemed to close in on him in his cold city home, but here in the wilderness, it was so pleasing to be with nature.

It was just as well, he thought since the animals were more elusive than usual. The beginning of the season brought him many furs, but the past month had seen little fruition. He felt maybe he should just go home as his food supply was dwindling. Wild game was his winter staple but with his luck, his provisions were a week away from being depleted.

As Jack stood out from the doorway of his cabin sipping his coffee, he heard a noise nearby. A very load rustling sound, a bear, he thought, an awakening bear from the winter slumber.

Jack fetched his gun and slowly walked toward the noise, and for some odd reason, he felt sluggish, if not drowsy. The bush was too thick for him to see what was making the noise. He slowly went around a giant old spruce as he tried to cover himself for a shot. Out of nowhere, a long limb knocked the gun off his hands, and there stood the most hideous native man he had ever seen.

"What the heck are you doing?" Demanded Jack as he stood in disbelief, "this is my private property, you bum."

The Native man grabbed the old white trapper by the throat and held him against a jack pine and queried in a slow gravelly voice, "kiwāpiskisin, tānihki? (You are white, why?)"

Jack's limp body offered no response. The hunting clothes he wore were a mystery to the giant as he tore them off effortlessly. Unlike the leather and fur clothing of his ancestors, the clothes were thin and easy to tear. As he stood tall and smelling the air and feeling the light breeze, he can feel the spirit of his enemy, the people of the community.

The reserve was wild and loud that morning. The heart of John Redbear, a Medicine Man, was torn. Torn between his love for his community members, and the malicious people they become when they consumed the poison of the snake spirit: alcohol. It was a feeling he felt many times before and may feel for the rest of his days. Then something in the distance, a feeling he felt when he was a boy, caught his attention. His heart shrunk in his chest and his fear raised the hair on his neck.

Jerry got ready for a trip across Sōniyāw Lake that morning. His wife and children were all giddy and cheerful. They survived another night of neighbors partying and knocking at their door. Now they were happy to be gone until the reserve settles down to a deathly quiet community with hangover and unfortunate hungry children roaming the dusty streets.

Jerry's wife Bethany had an old cabin built by her late father and they would delight in the trips they made to the pristine area of campfires and early morning, and late evening fishing. Berry picking and medicine gathering, taught the children responsibility and character. It was almost a resort type place except for no electricity or running water. Nature was their provider and with a little effort, they were happy to gather what they needed for water, heat, and food.

They loaded all the supplies they needed and off they went. The children were blessed to have had such caring guardians, unlike the children left behind to fend for themselves as their parents lay asleep or stumbled around in a drunken stupor.

John started to notice the feeling of dread in his inner core. He tried to recount the anxiety he felt as a child when he sat with his grandfather, who was getting ready to go into his sweat lodge to cleanse his mind body and spirit. His grandfather was to purify himself and John, for what was to come.

The spirit of the wihtikō lay near the outskirts of Sōniyāw Lake reserve. It was always near, and it has ravaged the community with malicious actions in the past. There was evil in the community, fueled by a lack of virtues and loss of harmony. The wihtikō evil spirit has used it as a gateway to return, his hunger grew and could only be satisfied by flesh and blood.

Days before his grandfather's ceremony, John would sit and chant with his drum. With his eyes closed, John's grandfather would be in a trance as he displayed immense concern on his face, as if in pain. The fast had lasted more than two days from what he remembers. The story his grandfather told him was ominous and that is what the old Medicine Man was going through. The evil they would be facing would be horrible and a thorough purification was essential.

Jerry and his wife enjoyed the weather as they fished like there was no tomorrow. Bethany had three fish in her bag and her husband had one. The children opted to stay at near the shore and try their aims in an archery contest with bows and arrows made by their father. With the sun getting lower in the sky, the couple start to make their way to shore with plenty of supper to go with their onions and potatoes.

Sōniyāw Lake Reserve begins to Stir

As the evening started, Sōniyāw Lake Reserve began to stir. Bootleggers had a fresh supply of alcohol because they knew the community was thirsty for one more round of boozing. Never mind the starving children, devastated homes, and broken hearts that they bring to their own people. Let the local leadership deal with the problems, they said. The snake spirit was well nourished in this community.

The leadership seemed deaf. The leadership heard the cries and the felt the pain of the people they represented. Community meetings often went unattended despite calls for such gatherings. The community members knew they needed help and made their pleas to leadership with such ferocity and passion, only to expect things to improve without any real heartfelt input from themselves.

Unfortunately, some of the leadership was in on the secret businesses of the despicable drug dealers and heartless bootleggers. One of the councillors was in cahoots with the gang leader that ran the underground businesses. It was a legal and moral violation of his duties to his suffering community. Many community members knew about the shady dealings, but they were too afraid to speak out. Not only would they potentially put themselves in danger but would possibly compromise their social assistance.

John and his grandfather

John and his grandfather were all packed for what seemed like for a long trip. His grandfather looked ready, despite the previous weeks fasting and preparing, he looked to be in a different state. Determination but with a false confidence that may have only been to show his grandson that he needs to be brave. John was worried.

They came upon the northern shores of a river that stretched out from east to west. They were greeted with marshland as far as the eye can see. The area in which they rested their bags that evening, showed the glades and the river shimmering in the sunlight. The landing in which they stood, was at the edge of the darkest parts of the boreal forest, with tall trees blocking the sunlight.

John's grandfather stood ready, closing his eyes as he waited for the evil to come. His grandfather stopped and opened his eyes. The wind had shifted from the west to south-west, and finally from the south. Southwind was like an invisible portal for travelling for a wihtikō. It is an advantage for the evil being.

Bethany was cooking the fresh catch of the day over a campfire. Her husband, Jerry, and their children tried some spear throwing to X shaped sticks on the ground, a game called "Indian Horseshoes." Bethany enjoyed the cool breeze from the north in the late spring day. Her thoughts were with her uncle, John Redbear, who had been acting strange in the last few days. She hoped he was healthy because the death of her father, John's brother, had hit him hard when he passed away several years earlier.

Councillor Brent and Shiv

The band councillor, Brent, and his cohort, the gang leader – Shiv, collaborated over instant messaging using fake accounts. They needed to meet regarding a shipment of illicit drugs and large quantities of hard liquor. Brent was getting paranoid over the possible discovery of his illegal actions from his collogues at the band office. Shiv assured him that nobody would dare come forward and implicate him because he has many boys that could take care of business if it happened.

Shiv had been the leader of his native gang, Rez Rage, for the last two years. Ironically, he was not even from the Rez or any reserve for that matter. He was an Urban Indian." He was small potatoes on the streets and was only useful as a runner who took all the risks for his leader in the so-called "hood" of Saskatoon, Saskatchewan. He was not even in the running for a leadership role in any of the shenanigans of his gang, he was a nameless thug who did the insignificant tasks and occasionally held up corner stores. He had too many failed attempts at robbing that he was too embarrassed to even mention his recent past to his devoted gang members. Here on the rez, he was a big man, he had followers that seemed to worship the ground he walked on and did as he demanded.

John Redbear Prepares

John Redbear lamented the death of his grandfather. The way he went down was for the good of the community. He knew that it was now his turn to prepare. He dug out the old and worn regalia of his beloved grandfather, among them, a bow and arrow and an old axe that was used to kill a wihtikō. The axe would come out last in his battle of mind, body, and spirit. The spirits needed to be observed and called, in what may be his last duty as a Medicine Man.

Fasting commenced immediately, as did his chanting. He went into his trances, so he could communicate with his ancestors. It would be a long three days. Purification was essential for this battle. His confidence was at an all-time low.

The wihtikō traveled wearily as he recognized the landscape of days past. His thoughts were jumbled, as if in a constant dream. The only thing certain was his hunger, and insatiable hunger that never went away. The warmth of the spring was a not welcome feeling but the cluster of ice on his back did well to sooth the discomfort. The dryness of his mouth was irritating as the wind blew through his teeth. No lips were present on his mouth, he had long eaten his own flesh before he came back. He missed a meal to ease the ravenous hunger when he did not eat Mr. Williams.

The wihtikō stopped to ascertain that it was the community members that he felt in his stomach. However, it was something else, not a Medicine Man or anything good, it was almost as dark as he was: the snake spirit. The snake spirit was alive in alcohol and would easily overtake holistic lifestyles to one of deprivation.

Sōniyāw Lake Reserve was again in the throes of wild festivity. Families that were together for a while were now ravaged into crowds of rowdy malice and negligence. The children were hungry and often hid from their drunken parents. Where grocery money should have gone, it went instead to alcohol and drugs. Little did the community know that they were feeding the evil that was coming closer and closer.

Bethany, Jerry and their two beautiful children had a great day. The time they spend together away from the riffraff was always a golden time. It was now time sleep, and their children laid on the bed they shared in the run-down, but comfy cabin. Bethany tucked the children in after a legend or two of wīsahkīcāhk and his many adventures.

Jerry put one more log in the fire before he called it a night. Bethany was already in bed reading a true story magazine. Jerry stopped by their bed before joining his wife and looked at her. "What?" Asks Bethany as she sees the look on his face.

"I love you so much." Stated Jerry.

"I love you too Jerry, now come to bed." Gushes Bethany, as she moves and uncovers the blanket to give him room.

Suddenly, there was a noise outside by the door. Jerry looked at Bethany with an assuring look that it was nothing. He slowly walked to the rickety door and yells out: "Hello! Who's out there? We're going to bed, and we don't want trouble and it's too late for company."

There was no sound after his request for identification, only the wind that seems to be picking up in strength. Jerry looks back at his wife, "There was nothing to worry abou…" Wack! An axe landed straight into the back of his head. Jerry stood for a while before falling forward.

"JERRY!" Screamed Bethany as the children started to cry, "DADDY!" They shriek.

The wihtikō broke through the door and stood up straight, looking at Bethany, then to her screaming children. He took the axe from Jerry's head and walks to the children and began hacking away. Bewildered, Bethany jumps on the wihtikō's cold back. Right away she felt the ice-cold cluster as she was thrown off beside the door. She got up and ran out the door as she heard the last cries of her children.

She found an old canoe near the shore and dragged it to the lake; she only managed to snatch an ancient canoe paddle that was well worn and thin from years of use. She pushed the canoe and jumped in and started paddling for her dear life. She looked back, only to hear the grotesque chewing of bloody flesh. She cried as she started paddling again and continued her escape. As she paddled hurriedly, she heard the water behind her, swishing and splashing. It was the wihtikō, waist deep in the water. He dove and swam swiftly toward Bethany, who was nearing the halfway mark of the lake to Sōniyāw Reserve.

As she tried to paddle harder, her paddle broke in half. She used the top part of the paddle to try and go faster as she heard the wihtikō coming closer behind her. The wihtikō managed to grasp the tail end of the canoe, an old canoe rickety enough to fall apart with one mighty blow from the monster legend.

Bethany succeeded in hitting the giant's hand off the tail end and then suddenly, bang! The wihtikō looked like he hit a wall. A barrier of some kind stopped him from continuing. Bethany looked back with astonishment. Her mouth wide open, she realized she must continue because whatever was holding back the cannibal, may weaken or break altogether.

On the third day of the fast, John knows he must start getting ready. The harmonious shield of protection was weaker than he thought it would be.

But it should come as no surprise because the harmony and love in the community was not strong with the people. Behaving the way, they do; it only helps to erode the shield and makes wihtikō even more dangerous.

Andrew was on his first term as chief. He knows Brent was an untruthful man who was just looking for a payday, even at the expense of the community. The previous chief, Adam, had been an honest man who finally stepped down after eleven 2-year terms and was ready to relax after serving his people for so long. Andrew knew he had to stay on top on things because he knew Brent had connections to an unsavoury group of misfits that sold marijuana and bootlegged hard liquor. Chief Adam did all he could to hold back Brent and his plans to make money from a proposed casino that would further ravage the community. Adam was no longer chief, he opted out of serving as an Elder to the Chief and Council board. He was tired from all the politics and the grief of his people. Andrew had a huge task in front of him.

An old man named PETER

Across the lake, an old man named Peter, was paddling along the beautiful shore. He had been canoeing along these shores for as long as he can remember. He and his grandfather went from lake to lake through the connecting rivers and stayed on many islands along the way. Oh, how he loved his grandfather, the old man was kind but stern. Peter learned how to shoot a gun, set snares and fish, all from his grandfather. He was grateful for all he learned from him.

Although he was never a religious man, he knew his grandfather believed in a higher power but did not really push it on him. The talks he had were more about the olden days of sweat lodges and many other traditional practices that were outlawed during his time. Churches were pushed on the community and his grandfather would go, just to appease the government and their funding. While funding was something Peter could not understand at the time, he went along with it. Peter himself attended church and prayed along with the people. When the praying was done, it was back to the lakes and the cabins and the lifestyle he loved so much.

He was coming near the cabin where his niece, Bethany and her family lived. They were such a good and decent family that Peter knew they would have tea ready for the weary traveler he was. Even though it was the break of dawn, they would be up and cooking breakfast while the children were asleep.

Strangely, not a stir could be heard as he pulled up his canoe onshore. He knew Jerry had bought a dog for his children and wondered why the canine did not at least bark, no less running up to greet him at the landing. Peter called out to Jerry and Bethany, but nobody answered, curious.

Peter figured the family did not show up yet, so he turned around and went back on his way. He stopped to consider going in to make fresh tea, but he decided not to. He wanted to get back to the reserve and relax on his 20-year-old couch and watch the one channel he can get on his massive 20-inch tube television.

As he paddled, he noticed a beaver bobbing quite a way from the shore, swimming in slow motion in little circles, as if to be biding his time and waiting for something. Peter found this to be very curious of a beaver's behaviour, as they usually moved along from one destination to another in their ever-busy lives. Suddenly the beaver stopped and slowly started going toward him. He found that even more curious as a beaver would either swim away, or dive right in and slap the water with his tail as a warning to the other beavers.

Peter did not need the fur of the animal, but he brought out his .22 to kill the beaver. He was sure Bethany, and her husband would appreciate some fresh meat for lunch. As the beaver got to about 30 feet from his canoe, he noticed the head was too big to be that of a beaver. He scrambled for his .303 as the protruding head got closer and at a faster pace. Three metres out he readied his gun and aimed directly at the head, which now had a human scowl to it. He prepares to pull the trigger, when suddenly the creature dives into the water. Peter was completely startled by the look he saw on the face of the beast, or whatever it was. His fevered anticipation of the creature emerging from the water, filled his mind in horror. He tried to clear his vision from the sweat and his mind from the disbelief he was experiencing.

Peter frantically looked around his canoe, with his gun pointing wherever he looked. Sweat poured down his face as his mind raced with fear. What could he have just seen? Why the frightening face on whatever the heck that was? Peter listened quietly. Not a peep or ripple of water was made. He held his gun across his chest, ready to point in any direction. His adrenalin has taken hold and he was ready for action. Flight was not an option when you are hindered by sitting in a canoe. he looked directly at the last place he saw the creature and slowly paned the area to the right toward the shore. Suddenly, he heard a small splash near the reeds and quickly points his body and gun toward it. It was just a northern pike, grabbing its prey at the surface of the murky water.

Peter breathed a sigh of relief. He slowly panned back toward the area and was relieved to see nothing, nothing at all. He puts his gun away and decides maybe he will go make a pot of tea to calm his nerves.

As he bends to grasp the paddle, he looks over the side of the canoe, only to see a horrible scowl in the water, before he could react, the creature grabbed him by the collar and pulled him in. Deep into the water he went with no struggle, frozen from fear he gives in without a fight. Bubbles rapidly rushed to the surface, until there was no more. Bethany has lost another family member without even knowing it.

With the south wind dying down. The wihtikō swam ashore and proceeded to walk the shore trails to the community. His destination was farther now since he must travel by foot. His hunger screamed with ravenous growls as he took his slow steps to where he was going. He noticed a back road and proceeded to follow that. The tall pine trees provided soothing cover from the rising sun. His constantly shifting eyes scan and pan all the plant life and surrounding area during his trek.

Outskirts of the Sōniyāw Lake Reserve

Way into the outskirts of the Sōniyāw Lake Reserve, two brand-new vehicles were parked, and two men were face to face arguing about getting the proper cut of profits. "I deserve half for covering up for your gang, Shiv," bellowed Brent," after providing most of the payment and lying to my colleagues, I demand half the money that you and your lads made off of my people."

"Ha-ha, YOUR people?" Mocks Shiv, as his wretched thugs laughed in unison. "Your people are more my people than they are yours. I bring what they want, and they are willing to do anything for me to get it. If the rest of your 'colleagues' knew what you were doing, you would be in jail."

"I want my half and we need to make a bigger order for next month, this petty cash was just not cutting for me. I have bills to pay and swiping it from the band funds was getting trickier. Chief Andrew was getting suspicious, and we may need to cut him in at some point" Cried Brent, "The chief and I are travelling to a funding meeting in the city in a couple of months and I need my relax time with more money."

"Not that I care but do the band members know you're a crook? You must have put more cash into a slot machine than you spend on housing and employment. If you want a bigger score than let me, take 65% of the revenue, I promise extra product next month that will get the poor souls more addicted and dependent on us. Something more than heavy alcohol and weak blunt. You and your so-called honest young chief will have so much more than you can imagine."

Several metres from where they stand, they hear a noise, a shuffling of leaves and twigs. "Who's there?" Shiv yells, "you better come out buddy, or I'll take you out man."

"Cheese and rice!" Cried Brent, "I'm getting out of here, I can't be seen with you thugs."

Brent covered his head with his jacket as he ran to his brand-new SUV, as he neared the door, he heard a shot. He turned around and saw nothing. "Shiv? Where are you?"

Rustling started again in the wooded area, "Did you get him Shiv?" Brent asked. He heard grunting and a disgusting slurping noise. "Shiv, what are you doing to him? Let's get out of here before more people come." Brent fumbled with his cell phone to turn on the flashlight app and dropped it. "Oh no, this cell cost the band $1000."

Brent bent to pick up the phone and brushed the dirt off it. He stopped to listen as he turned the phone flashlight app toward the woods. He called out, "Shiv! Are you there?" No answer. He quickly climbed into his band paid vehicle and drove off. He thought of calling the real police but thought better of it. He does not want to be caught associated with such a vile group of people.

Chief Andrew was in a bind. His scheduling of a community meeting was at a bad time: the day after welfare day. He had seen enough suffering and many of the sober people were pleading with him to do something. He vowed to act, but he knew he would need the cooperation of the people who drink. They would have to voluntarily seek treatment. That meant being shipped off to a centre where they could recover and learn about staying sober. The bootleggers were another problem. He knew some of the tribal police were taking bribes and he knew that Brent was involved somehow with the bribery.

This community meeting must happen today, he thought to himself. He knew it would be very difficult to discuss the problems with the community and the opposition would be smirking at him for attempting such a conference.

Bethany was hurting, emotionally, physically, and mentally. Spiritually, she was praying for strength. She knew what she saw at their cabin, her uncle used to tell stories of an evil entity: wihtikō. She had to get to her community but with a broken paddle, she travelled at a snail's pace. She was tired, she needed strength. She knew there was supposed to be a community meeting today, however, she did not plan to attend. Her husband did not attend those meetings because he felt they were a waste of time, and nothing was ever done about the drunken partying. They had both heard stories about their crooked Councillor and did not trust the new chief.

She wanted to see her uncle; he would know what to do about the cannibal. It was an evil that cannot be killed from a bullet or from just any man. Only the strength of our ancestors can defeat the wihtikō. She lamented the times she would rather play than to listen to all the teachings and stories from her uncle. She used to see the disappointment in the face of John Redbear, as she pranced away to see her friends.

She paddled along toward the point as she grieved all the carelessness she had done in her childhood. Now she needed her uncle more than ever. As Bethany made her way around the point, she saw the familiar sight of dim lights of her community across the lake.

Chief Andrew Starts the Community Meeting

Chief Andrew sat at his table facing members of his community. Many of the community members were quiet and some were obviously hungover. Chief Andrew stood up to greet the twenty or so attendants who bothered to show up. He forced a smile and told them that he knew what problems have been facing the community. He informed them that there had been rumours of corruption in the band and that he was doing what ever he could to get to the bottom of it. His main concern now, was the drinking and drug abuse prevalent in the community.

He laid out the plan for treatment and how the only way for the membership to heal was to willingly seek treatment. He had organized with the local health centre to make up application forms for the trips to treatment centres. He explained that nobody can be forced to go to the centres, they would need to go voluntarily.

A representative from the health centre was asked by Chief Andrew to attend the meeting and provide the needed forms for the treatment centre trips. The representative stood up to speak when somebody started banging on the door to the community hall. "It's open," yelled Chief Andrew.

A disheveled woman came bursting in, "Help, you have to help my family!" She screamed.

Chief Andrew immediately rushed to the woman and asked her, "What happened? Where is your family?" Chief Andrew barely recognized her; it was Bethany.

Bethany explained as best as she could about the events that happened to her and her family across the lake. She muttered something about a monster and how he was on his way to the community to kill everybody.

Chief Andrew was shocked by her story. He quickly rallied all community members who had guns and boats. They were going to find the culprit and apprehend him or kill him if they had to. The tribal police were called up, but they showed up outside the community hall with Brent already to roll.

Brent ran up to Chief Andrew, "Andrew, you have to come with us, the tribal police have found the remains of some thugs about five kilometres west from the community near the lake. It looks like they were ripped apart and maybe even eaten." Cried Brent.

"What?" Asked Andrew, "Why didn't you call the police for assistance?"

"Well," stammered Brent, he knew he could be compromised if the real police showed up, "I just thought we could take care of it before we called them. We don't wanna be seen as incompetent and lazy."

Andrew bit his lip and suspected Brent's involvement. The councillor was too close to the thugs to involve the real police and so he called up his crooked tribal force.

Wihtikō came to a landing and waded into the lake. He started swimming to the community that was seemingly calling his name. He swam along for many strokes, only to find that the shield was still active, but was apparently weakening.

Chief Andrew and Brent Gather the Membership

Andrew and Brent gathered the members who were willing to take part in the man hunt. The tribal police decide to show some unity with the band and round up the tribal outboard boats with their 60 HP motors. The group banded together at the main landing of the community and discussed the plan at hand on how to deal with the killer. "We will head straight to the family's cabin and troll the area to find the killer." Shouted a tribal officer.

"The killer could have gone back to shore for all we know and maybe could have drowned." Said Andrew.

"There is no way that monster could have drowned, he might even be at shore nearby." Brent replied.

"That halfway mark is a long swim to our community Brent," Andrew declared, "Bethany told us that the killer stopped half-way, chances are, he was too tired to continue."

"She also said he was prevented by some type of 'shield' he could not get past. The tribal police said they found the remains on the west side of the lake. He could be swimming from that side of the lake too." Explained

Brent, without giving away his knowledge of the events that took place at the outskirts of the community.

"What does that have to do with this situation Brent? Bethany's family was attacked at the north of the community, around that point." Andrew Clarified, as he motioned with his hand the general area where the killer would most likely be. "We can't worry about a group of thugs when sensible people from our community have been hurt. Now let's get going before it gets too late."

John lived on the east side of the Sōniyāw Lake. There was only so much goodness in the community to keep the shield up. It weakened as he stalled from the inevitable confrontation. His spirit was ready, but his body was weak. He would need to rest soon.

Chief Andrew's search party cruised along the water at full throttle, four boats with three people to each one. They came near the half-way point and started to spread out to the north and west. The boat most western of the lake slammed into something and came to a dead stop. The driver and both passengers went flying off the boat and splashed loudly onto the water. One of them bobbed up, "What the heck did we hit?" He demanded to know. Suddenly, he got pulled into the water and never surfaced again. The other two boaters that were floating helplessly, were also pulled under as they screamed for help.

The wind shifted from the south once again. The boaters did not notice the warm breeze because their racing horrified thoughts were set on something else. The capsized boat was dented badly at the front hull. There was no reefs or logs to be seen. They could not even fathom what pulled the capsized boaters in.

The south winds started to pick up as the lake showed little ripples going over the surface. The remaining three boats and their commuters looked around in silence with guns locked and loaded. They could hear water trickling on the hull of one of the boats and all parties nervously point their guns toward the noise. "Come out, whoever you are!" Shouted Andrew.

"Or whatever you are." Exclaimed Brent, breathing slowly as his gun shook in his hands.

Suddenly, the killer furiously rose from the lake and the splashed water all over the boaters. The tribal police started shooting in a frenzy toward the monster but were shooting each other instead. The wihtikō releasing his special power of gliding in the south wind dropped down to the water and stayed submerged. Only two boats remained with passengers. Brent and Andrew were on each boat with band members frantically panning the waters with their guns. "We need to get out of here." Brent cried, as he held his shotgun.

"Okay," Andrew said in a shaky voice, "let's get ready, drivers put your guns down slowly and get ready to go full throttle." The drivers reluctantly set their guns beside themselves and proceeded to grip the throttles of their outboard motors. As the first boat with Brent turns quickly to toward the community, the wihtikō burst out of the water in front of them and wacked the head off Brent as the boat cruised under the monster. Brent's headless body went flying to the boat driver and knocked him overboard. Andrew and his driver hit the capsized driver of the first boat and ripped the face and scalp of the driver off and did not survive. Andrew and his driver continued to cruise toward the community and left the others behind, including the wihtikō.

The wihtikō floated in place as he stared at the boat getting smaller as it went further and further toward the community. In his insatiable hunger for more flesh, he had not noticed right away. The shield was gone.

John woke up from a restful sleep. He knew his slumber would take down the shield, but he needed his sleep, perhaps undeserved sleep. He had put the community in jeopardy. He felt the evil presence of the embodied evil near the community. His senses were sharp, his body was old but nimble and his mind was clouded with fear, but he was determined. He started his walk to the community. Humble, but confident.

Wihtikō glided gently toward the village. His sight was filtered through a blood red haze. He scanned the shoreline as his heartbeat grow louder from the sheer hunger. He felt the fresh flesh that lay ahead. Nearing the shoreline, he targeted a run-down house that looked nothing like the teepees of the past. He touched down at ankle deep water and proceeded to walk toward the house that had much activity going on.

Chief Andrew and his surviving crew were up in arms at the band hall. They knew it was an ancient evil that has somehow come back from the past and they heard the stories all their lives about the wihtikō. They could not kill the cannibal with bullets, and they had little knowledge of their own traditional medicine. They knew time was running out, they needed to be on their way to the shore to wait for the wihtikō.

John Redbear got to the main landing of the community and saw a figure walking towards a house. He knew right away it was the evil cannibal. He called out to his nemesis, "wihtikō! ōtī. (Over here)." Immediately, the confidence he felt earlier, left him.

The wihtikō turned his head and knew right away who was calling out to him. A gristly grin went over his ratchet face and started walking toward the weak medicine man: "kikitimakanatin pacapis. Iyawis oko nihithawak ika ahpo iki wicihisocik. (I feel sorry for you, old man. All these people cannot even help themselves."

John stood speechless. After his rest and his spirit purification, he was brimming with confidence and determination. He was feeling the strength of his ancestors, but then, he felt abandoned. He would have to do this on his own. He understood what his late grandfather had to go through. The drain he saw on his grandfather's face in days past became very real and painful. How could he do it alone, he thought. He had no more time to prepare. It was time.

The wihtikō stared at the medicine man. John stood 50 metres from the atrocious being. He drew his bow and arrow and shot him: he missed. The wihtikō did not need to move out of the way. He could smell the fear of the old man and started walking straight for him. John was taken aback by his bad aim. He rarely missed a target, but his fear was an enormous distraction to his once sharp senses. Senses that were now at an all-time low. At 30 metres, John drew another arrow, his last chance to somehow decapitate his enemy. The wihtikō was just 10 metres away when, BLAM!

Chief Andrew and his squad had arrived just in time to shoot the wihtikō on the shoulder. The wihtikō, quickly turned to the group and roared at Andrew and his cohorts. Unfazed, he started walking toward them. Andrew was in shock; the gunshot barely fazed the monster and only damaged the blood soaked hide he was wearing. One of Andrew's band members shouted, "I got this, and went running up to the wihtikō and pointed his shotgun to his face, BLAM! The wihtikō backed up a couple of feet. He shook his head but only to shake off the buckshot from his face and ragged hair. The band member stood in terror as his gun was taken away and used to bash his head in.

Andrew prepared to shoot the wihtikō with his gun when the monster yanked the gun off his hands. Wihtikō was about to make his move when he suddenly stopped and grimaced a horrible scowl. An arrow had struck him on the right shoulder. John Redbear had collected his thoughts enough to steady a shot with his bow.

The wihtikō's right arm was now useless. The arrow had medicine that was harmful for the evil cannibal. His anger was elevated, his emotional level was increased, but physically, he had depreciated.

John Redbear felt he had a chance. The wihtikō was weaker. John pulled out his old hatchet and stood head-to-head with his enemy. Wihtikō tried to swipe John with his left arm and nearly caught his hair. John's reflexes were still sharp enough but just barely. He stepped back as adrenalin raced through his body. John swung with all his might toward the neck of wihtikō. Wihtikō's reflex response was still superior and ducked down. He jumped up in the air as the south wind was still going strong and flew overhead of John. John grabbed the dangling right arm of the wihtikō and slung him to the ground using his left hand. Wihtikō fell on his ice-clustered back writhing in pain. John quickly straddled the cannibal and lopped off the head of his adversary. John collapsed from sheer exhaustion. As he lay on the ground with his heart still racing, he yelled out to Chief Andrew: "Chief! Make a big fire, quickly." Chief Andrew knew from the legends he heard growing up. They needed to burn up the evil being to an absolute crisp, or the evil would find a way to come back.

Bethany sat beside her uncle as he rested in his cabin. John Redbear was happy to be near a family member as he had been alone for too long. In the days ahead, Bethany stayed with her uncle as she mourned the death of her family and dealt with the trauma of the past week. It took two days of a constant bon fire to finally burn the wihtikō to a crisp. She was happy to have her uncle John and vowed to learn her culture this time. Chief Andrew still had the community's problems to deal with, but he worked out a plan to bring more sobriety for his people. The recent deaths of many of his people at the hands of the evil wihtikō, was adding to the suffering of the community. With much of the wickedness gone, the community stood a chance at a better future.

Chapter Three

Into the Life's Circle

The old man sat on his bed and cried for his late wife. It was a full year since she had died, and she was all he could think about. Twenty-three years of marriage into his then 64 years was wonderful but now she was gone.

The macaroni and cheese were done, and he served himself. His wife used to cook the most delicious meals for him. His long workdays would be rewarded with another scrumptious supper, a supper fit for a king.

They married late in life because they could never stay together long enough to commit to each other. It was only much later that they decided to settle down. Their daughter was born a couple years after they married, and they couldn't believe they didn't start sooner. They missed out on so much.

Hank decided he was going to visit an old Indigenous friend, John Red Bear. It had been a while since he saw anybody, and figured John was just as good a host as any. They used to work in the mines together until they were around forty years, and by then their bodies had had enough.

"Hello Hank! It's been a long time," John greeted him.

"John ol' pal, it's good to see you."

Hank and John sat and reminisced about the old days and how their fathers would not allow them to see each other.

"The white man's child will corrupt you, son" John's father would say, and Hank's dad didn't want him hanging around those "darn wagon-burners."

The old friends shared some good laughs until John asked Hank how he had been doing since Abigail died.

Poor ol' Hank realized he hadn't even thought of his wife during this time. Shame filled his heart as he felt he had betrayed his late wife's memory. "John, it seems to never get easier," John said. He wept, "It was only just today I haven't thought of her for a mere few minutes, but for the past year, she been all I've thought about."

John felt the sorrow in his friend's heart. He could only imagine what Hank was going through because he never got married. His devotion was to his ancestral spirituality. He had the option of finding a wife, but he did not want to put her through the negligence of being a medicine man's wife. His time would always be for his people, many of whom no longer shared his beliefs.

He had not done any kind of ceremony for a long time. Nobody came to him with offerings of tobacco or spiritual healing. He longed for the connection to his spirituality. The few people who practiced with him visited less often. He sensed the need to reach the spirits again.

Hank got up and thanked John for his hospitality. He looked out at the horizon, and it reminded him of the long walks he used to take with

Abigail. If he ever wanted a time to stay where it was, it would be when they walked and talked, and time stood still.

John Red Bear was on a mission. He would find a path for his friend into the afterlife. It would be seamless and painless for his long-time friend. He did not want Hank to suffer any longer. His broken heart was not healing, and a ceremony would provide a safe journey for his friend.

John made the necessary arrangements with what was left of his tribesmen with whom he practiced. The drum songs were sung, and the offering of the tobacco made.

In his bed, Hank tossed and turned as he struggled to sleep. His mind raced to a distant beat with no relief forthcoming to his endless agony.

The next day, John Red Bear felt he had accomplished what he set out to do. He allowed his friend to skip to the next world without death and he would be with Abigail.

In the horizon, John saw a visitor coming his way. He thought it might be his grandson. John waved to the coming figure and realized it was Hank.

"John, my friend, I've come back for your great brew," Hank said.

John just stood in disbelief, "Hank… you're alive."

"Just barely, but one cup of 'Indian' java should liven me up", Hank quipped.

"Of course, Hank" said John as he invited his friend into his tipi.

"What the heck are you doing in this pointed tent John?" Hank asked, as he took the freshly brewed coffee in his hand.

"Oh, this I'm just trying to feel some history. It's good to go back sometimes," John said.

As the old friends sat and exchanged stories, John thought to himself that maybe his ceremony brought relief to the hopelessness Hank had been feeling. Maybe Hank didn't need to go to the next world just yet. The look on Hanks's face was one of calmness. John was happy for his friend.

"Abigail should be getting here soon." said Hank.

"What? Abigail is coming?" John exclaimed.

"My one and only" said Hank proudly, "oh, there she is, right on time, we're actually here to pick you up." explained Hank.

"Pick me up? Where are we going?" asked John.

"You know where we're going, all three of us."

John was bewildered, what was Hank talking about? Did his old friend finally lose it? Did so many months of grieving get to the old guy?

"You're looking all peaceful there." said Hank, as he pointed to the side of the tipi.

John looked to see a person on the ground. He went over to the body, of who he thought was one of his tribesmen. John saw himself on the ground.

He realized that when he woke that morning, there was nobody else around. He had been with several of his tribe members overnight to prepare for the ceremonies. As he looked around outside, he noticed that only his tipi was erect, but his house and other belongings were nowhere to be seen.

Behind John Red Bear's house, close to his sweat lodge, a young man wept over his grandfather's body. The body was still warm. He had tried to revive him with his CPR training but to no avail. John Red Bear was still in his ceremonial regalia and held a well-worn drum in his hand. The other tribesmen came running over. "He was still chanting when we went home." One of them said, "He refused to stop when we asked him to, he was so determined."

John's grandson was only there to tell his grandfather the news of his old friend Hank passing away in his sleep. He was there to see Hank being taken away by the ambulance and was now waiting for the same thing to happen to his grandfather. Hank's daughter already got the phone call. John never had a phone; he was always so old fashion.

"Is there anything we can do?" the tribesman said.

John's grandson got up to give one last song for his grandfather and his friend, to bid them a happy journey to the Spirit World.

Just beyond the horizon, under the brightness of the sun, John, Hank, and Abigail, begin their journey to the next world. No more pain, no more sorrow, with only the hope of a new beginning, in the never-ending circle of life.

Chapter Four

Kipochh the Wanderer

Long ago in Native culture, there was a complete idiot whose name was Kipochh the wanderer. He was loosely tied to any other people and did whatever he wanted to do. Many times, he only got himself in trouble.

One day, Kipochh was walking through the woods, and came upon a meadow, an immense grassy field. He liked the way the strong breeze felt in his face, and as he looked up, he noticed an eagle gliding in the wind. He wondered how it would feel to fly like a bird. It must be a great feeling to fly around so freely, he thought.

He decided to find out and asked the eagle: "Mikisiw," he called out," come down and tell me how it feels to fly."

The eagle felt quite annoyed at the intrusion and screamed back: "It feels great, but you will never really know, so just leave me alone." The eagle asserted and flew further away to avoid the pest yelling at him.

Kipochh jumped up and down and demanded the eagle to come back, but the bird didn't listen. Kipochh calmed down but he was still determined to find out how flying felt.

He went back into the woods "how in the world will I ever find out?" he thought. Just then, he saw some chickadees resting on a branch. He asked them the same thing he asked the eagle, but the small birds ignored him and flew to another branch. Kipochh persistent as he was, walked over to the other branch and asked them: "Just tell me a few things about it." The birds looked at each other and smiled: "Catch us if you can, Ha! Ha!" the birds chirped and flew out of sight.

Kipochh felt sad, he was so eager to find out how it felt to fly, but he would never get any help from the snobby birds.

During a long sorrowful walk, Kipochh came upon a lake and noticed a pelican floating happily on the water. Kipochh stood on the shoreline and had a great idea. He jumped in the lake and dove until he was just under the pelican. He reached up and grabbed the pelican's legs. He hung on and tried to provoke the big bird to fly away, instead, he pulled the legs right off. The pelican flew a little way and then died on the water.

Kipochh swam back to shore and was very disappointed that he couldn't experience the thrill of flying. He then had a thought, the combined weight of him and the large bird was too much to become airborne. All he would need to do was use the wings himself. The pelican's wings might be large enough to hold him up and glide through the air.

He swan back out the dead pelican and dragged it to shore. He cut off the wings and tied them to his arms. He needed a high place to jump from. As he searched for high grounds, he thought of how exciting and fun it would be to fly through the sky.

He searched for many hours and could not find a hill or cliff high enough for his maiden flight. He decided to look for the tallest tree he could find. Moments later, he found one.

The tree was very tall, tall enough for Kipochh to glide for a long, long time. He started to climb and as he started to get winded, he looked down and noticed just how high the tree really was. He didn't care though because he determined to fly.

He stood on the highest branch that could hold his weight. He jumped away the tree and spread his wings. The feeling was surreal, magic, it was wonderful. That is until he started to fall. He had only flown two feet away from the tree. As he fell, he grabbed out for the branches and managed to slow his fall. He hit the ground with a loud thud and got up holding his sore back.

He looked at the place he fell and up at the tree he fell from. Kipochh decided then and there that he would never again try to do what only certain animals are supposed to do.

As he walked, he came upon a river, and as he stood on the riverside, he observed the fish swimming by. He wondered how it would feel to swim like a fish.

Chapter Five

Kipochh Saves The Sun (According To Him)

Kipochh the wanderer strolled through the meadow and loved the feel of the warm breeze. A sunny afternoon always brought a smile to his face and made him forget everything.

One day, he thought about how beautiful the daylight was and wondered where the light came from. He looked up at the sun and he pondered the source of power in the great ball of fire. In villages across the land there would be fire-keepers who kept the blazes going so they don't shut off, but who kept the sun on fire?

He just had to know, somebody knows what's going on and he was going to find out. His plan was to check out a few of the villages and ask how and why certain people were chosen and when they take their breaks.

He saw a small village of Cree living on the great plains, many of the women were busy tending to hides and teaching their children how to do various tasks needed for daily survival and sustenance. Kipochh was naturally curious about this and wondered how they could be so disciplined and determined to keep up the harmony that the tribe enjoyed. Everybody did their part but the one he was most interested in was the Firekeeper, keeper of the flames.

He didn't see any kind of fire keeping within the village and the only camp fires were for smoking meat and hides. He then noticed a small lodge at the edge of the river. It was more like a tipi than a lodge but there was definitely smoke coming out of it. This was it, he thought.

He crept to the tipi and gently rapped on the buffalo hide covering, "Hello, is anyone there?" he asked. "Who's there?" the person inside responded.

"It's Kipochh, I want to know how you keep the fire going,"

"Please leave me alone and get away from here, you're only going to mess things up, I heard about you."

Hearing this, Kipochh started kicking the tipi and yelling, "LET ME SEE WHAT YOU DO!"

The person inside started yelling, "No you idiot, I am the keeper of the flame, the flame in the sky."

Kipochh stopped, "keeper of the flame in the sky?" he repeated, "YOU are the one who keeps the sun and it's fire? Why are you the only one here, is it even safe here?"

"It's been safe here for 100 years, roots along the sacred river are the ingredients that keeps me well enough and strong enough to keep the fire alive. This is my last summer, and then I must pass on this gift to another."

Kipochh decided that maybe he can be the new keeper of the flames, "O gifted one, I volunteer my life to the flame in the sky." Kipochh proclaimed proudly.

"Ha ha, you? I don't think so Kipochh, you can't even take care of yourself." The Firekeeper, who is not supposed to be bothered by anybody at all, started laughing hardily and forgot his time to sprinkle sacred herbs into the fire to continue the flame.

This responsibility, which has been in existence since the world began, had never been taken for granted or treated with such thoughtlessness. "No, the herbs! Kipochh, you made me forget the herbs, get out of here, I have to try and regain the flame."

Kipochh ran into the woods where he always sought seclusion from the inconveniences of life and dealing with other people. Many times, it was just to get away from the trouble he had caused but it was safe from harm nonetheless.

Suddenly, the sun started flickering like a campfire being blown from the harsh winds of the plains. Kipochh was startled by this and needed to get away from the trouble he had caused, but where would he go? The sunshine always brought a ray of hope from past troubles, but it was now in danger of shutting out.

Quickly he had to figure something out. What could he do? What was the Firekeeper talking about, sacred herbs? What sacred herbs? He knew about rat root and Labrador tea leaves but what did the Firekeeper need to ignite the power of sunshine?

He was running out of time and had no time to think so he grabbed whatever plant species he could find along the way to the tipi. He grabbed leaves; berries, roots, and soil, there had to be something the Firekeeper could use.

When he got to the tipi, the Firekeeper was panicking and pacing along the river, he was frantically snapping up whatever roots from under the willow trees. He saw Kipochh running towards him holding a bushel of plants and yelling out to him, "I GOT SOME MEDICINE!"

When Kipochh got near the Firekeeper, the Firekeeper knocked the bushel down and started rummaging through it. "YES, THAT'S IT!" he shouted.

He went running into the tipi and caught the last spark with the Labrador tea leaf, just enough to spark it up and then the rest of the herbs could stoke the flame and then to a perfect campfire.

The sun was saved and mother earth had her warmth secured.

As Kipochh was wandering through the land once again, after saving the world (according to him), he wondered what caused the rain to come down.

Chapter Six

Kipoch Mounts a Ride

Kipoch was wandering the plains and spoke with many different tribes who told tales of men mounted on the backs of large animals. The animals were said to be like large dogs, "mistatimwak" they called them. Many distances away they traveled and moved faster and with more supplies.

Kipoch wanted in on this, if it means not walking long distances, then even better. He asks the different people about the beasts and he got different answers. Were they like bears or moose, or maybe buffalo? He was given many different answers. He just had to find out for himself.

He walks for hours when he decides to at least try mounting what he can find. Since he was in the woodland area, he figured it have to be the maskwa (bear) or mōswa (moose), or how about the mahikan (wolf). However, the wolves liked him but they would never let him mount them and he didn't want the cunning animals on his bad side. Bears and moose he didn't care for.

A maskwa might maul him to death like they have done to so many humans in the past, but he knew he had to try something. He noticed an iyāpīw – bull moose and an onīcāniw – cow moose. It was toward the end of rutting season. The bull moose had been fighting a good while to get where he is today with the cow he was with.

The bull looked tired, but he may still be in fighting mode. There is no way he would mess with that bull. The cow, however, seems to be more passive and is always feeding and sitting around. If he could get close enough and if the bull is not around, he may actually get a chance to ride his animal. Then it was decided, Kipoch will become a modern Indian today.

The cow is sitting around as usual, doing something but who knows what. Lo and behold, the bull was gone, and the cow was nodding off. It was his chance to make things happen, specifically his boring life.

Kipoch sneaks over to the cow who is laying blissfully on the grass, for now. As Kipoch looks on with his googly eyes, he tries not to make a sound. He gets within two metres and then suddenly, he makes a running dash for the back of the moose. Haaa! He yells, as the cow jumps right up and tries bucking Kipoch off her back.

Later that day, Kipoch woke up from the leafless thorn bush, he gets up and looks gravely at the moose standing so tall and arrogant. He walks along the edge of the forest and sees his next ride "It will be safer mounting the maskwa."

Chapter Seven

Moon Rising

Steve was walking to school and noticed his friends Tom and Chris were talking. Steve knew how Tom was and that Tom was probably doing all the talking while Chris stood there nodding his head. He soon came upon them. "Hey guys, what's happening?"

"Didn't you hear? There was a killing last night." Tom says, "I hear an animal attacked them and ate them."

"What? Who?" Steve says.

"Mike and Paul," Toms says, "I guess they were out on the edge of town late last night."

"Holy Man! What kind of animal?"

"They say it might be a bear or maybe even a wolverine."

Steve's mouth hangs open as he tries to absorb the terrible news. Tom looks at Steve curiously, "Well?"

"Well what?" Steve asks.

"Well, what do you think?"

"I think I'm really shocked, I think I'm saddened. What the Hell do you think I think? This is serious stuff!" Steve says, as he shakes his head in disbelief . "Two of our classmates died last night," Steve continues, "and all you care about is 'what I think,'" Steve decides to go farther, "It must be great for you to have something so interesting to talk about, but you should show more consideration."

Tom stands there dumbfounded and feels ashamed that he even asked such a discerning question, for awhile anyway. "Chris what do you think?" Tom says as catches Chris off guard.

"I ...What do you mean?" Chris says.

"About the killings."

"I already told you." Chris says awkwardly.

"Well tell me again" insists Tom.

"Well whatever Steve said I guess."

"That's not ...What you ... oh forget it, I have to go talk to some other people, bye!." Tom leaves and immediately comes upon a group of people to talk to.

Steve and Chris start walking to their classes. "So Chris, how are you holding up?"

"I'm alright I guess."

"That's strange, I thought you were good friends with Mike and Paul?"

"I was, " explains Chris, "I just don't know how to react to the news I guess."

"I'm sorry, I didn't mean to say you didn't care or anything." Apologizes Steve.

"I'll be fine." Assures Chris.

A few weeks pass as Steve thinks about his little discussion with Chris that afternoon. Chris always seems to be so quite and unwilling to debate about anything. He more or less agrees with everything his friends have to say. Tom is another story. He always finds something to talk about, and the newer and more interesting it is, the better.

Tom sits at home thinking about the massacre that happened almost a month ago. He just feels he has to know what happened. Suddenly, he gets a great idea.

The next day at school, Tom goes around asking if anyone wants to join him on an investigation of the killings that happened. He pretty much covered everybody except Steve and Chris. Steve and Chris come out of the school at home time and see Tom standing on the sidewalk staring at them. "What's up with you?" Asks Steve.

"I need your help," Tom says, "I can't find anyone who wants to help me out."

"With what?" Questions Steve, as he looks at Tom suspiciously.

"To investigate the killings last month."

"What? Are you out of your mind?" Asks Steve, "You know it was an animal who did the killing, not some crazy murderer."

"How can we be sure, man? The moon was full that night. I checked the calendar."

"So it was a cannibal or something? Maybe the Wehtigo? Or maybe it was the Bigfoot coming to eat the Indians during the full moon." Steve laughs

"I'm thinking it was a guy who has a vicious dog with him, maybe two vicious dogs."

"Yeah there are alot of mutts on the reserve, but they're all too damn stupid to kill their own prey."

"Maybe their owner is a loony person who just loses it during the full moon."

"I don't know Tom. It sounds to hard to believe."

"Remember a few months back? There was another killing that was very similar."

"Yeah. It was the old wino guy. I heard about it. He was a loner from another reserve. Nobody even bothered to identify the poor old' guy's body."

"You know what's interesting about that?" Asks Tom as he anticipates Steve's obvious answer.

"What?"

"The moon was full."

"The moon was full?"

"The moon was totally full." Explains Tom with a smile on his face.

"Just the same I'd rather not go with you. It's too stupid."

"Well Chris will come with me. Won't you Chris?"

"I ... don't .."

"Come on Chris don't be like that."

"I ..."

"Chris, you don't have to go with him." Says Steve.

"I ... Okay, I'll go Tom, but only because I want to know what happened to my friends."

"Right on Chris, I knew I could count on you."

"I guess I'll go too." Steve says, "But only so you don't get Chris in trouble."

"Great, we'll take off about eleven, I'll call you guys anyway."

"Tonight?" Asks Steve.

"Tonight's the full moon, see ya."

That night, Tom lead Steve and Chris to the edge of town at an old parking lot where the killings took place. They found a place just off the lot where it was bushy enough to hide them as they waited. After a while, they waited some more. "...What are we supposed to be looking for?" asks Chris.

"You have to be quiet Chris, the killer might hear you." Tom explains "The moon is at its fullest and my BB gun is pumped and ready."

"Why did you bring that anyway?" Steve says, "If we do see something and you shoot it, you'll probably just piss it off some more."

"Be quiet now." Toms whispers.

The boys wait quietly for another hour before anyone says anything. "Guys I'm starting to get hungry." Chris says,"Shouldn't we go home now?" he asks.

"Yeah Tom it's almost 1 am, we should get going soon." Steve adds.

"Lets give it one more hour guys," Tom pleads, "I just know something's bound to show up."

"Thirty minutes, and I'm gone." Steve says.

As Tom and Steve look on intensively, Chris starts to wonder if its a good idea to ask if the guys have any snacks on them. He decides not to bother. Chris is always too shy to impose on anybody. He often wonders how his friends can be so brave and why he is so timid. He thinks back of the times he just could not say no to his friends, including Mike and Paul. For some reason, he starts to remember vividly where he was when the killings happened. It was becoming clear, whereas before, he couldn't even remember where he was that evening. "Guys, I've got to tell you something." Chris says.

"Chris be quiet," Tom demands, "the killer is coming."

"Where?" Steve asks surprisingly.

"Right there." Tom says as he slowly points to just off the side of the lot.

The creature slowly walks toward the middle of the lot where a big garbage can was resting. Tom gets his gun ready and takes careful aim. POP!, goes the BB gun as the startled creature runs off. Tom and Steve jump up and dash for the parking lot. Chris, for some reason, starts to feel a deep hunger. His veins starts to pulse all over his body.

At the garbage bin, Tom and Steve look toward the bush dumbfounded. Why would a bear come out during the full moon? They thought.

As they headed back to their spot, they heard moans and gasps from where Chris was lying. "Are you okay Chris?" Asks Steve. But all they hear is painful noises.

Chris starts to realize that hair is forcing through his clothes and claws through his shoes, and as he begins to settle down, the sight of fresh game stands before him.

The next day at school, Chris notices a commotion among the students outside the building. He over hears a group's discussion. One of the students sees him and runs over to him. "Hey Chris did you hear? There was a killing last night."

Chapter Eight

Chris and Amanda

On a late sunny afternoon, a boy named Chris and his sister, Amanda, were listening in on their parents discussing their plans to go out for the evening. Bingo was the topic at hand, the parents were considering the possible babysitters they had in mind, and they had a large list of rotating potentials.

The kids were familiar with all the babysitters, and they had their favorites and not-so favorites. They listened intently as the parents settled on Charlene, a mild-mannered but absent-minded teenager.

The kids were happy with the choice because they knew Charlene would pay no mind to what they did and sometimes to where they were.

The kids were in the playroom while the babysitter danced by herself in the living room. It seemed like the best time to plan an adventure, which usually meant a game of hide n' seek outside.

Chris turned to his sister and said: "Don't you think this is getting boring?"

"What do you mean?" said Amanda.

"We been doing this same ol' adventure since we 5 and 7, but we are 7 and 9 now, so we should think of something else."

"How about hopscotch, that's a fun game." Beamed Amanda.

"No, let's pretend to be like our ancestors, the Woodland Cree, and explore the wilderness."

"The Wilderness?" said Amanda, "But we'll get lost"

"Oh no, just in the backyard, sister" explained Chris, "There's trails to follow and we can always see the house."

"Okay."

So off they went to the backyard, which on the reserve, meant there was plenty of trees. The bush had many old trails in it, they were probably made long before there were houses in that particular area.

Chris turned to Amanda and told her to start counting on the mītos (popular tree), and not to peek as he assured her that he wasn't going to go very far.

When Amanda got to ten, she looked around and yelled: "You better not have gone too far!"

She began to creep up to some nīpisiya (red willows), where she thought her brother might be. She jumped to the side of the brush and said: "I got you!" but he wasn't there.

In the distance, she heard a stick crack, she yelled out: "Is that you Chris? That better be you, Chris!"

There was no response, but the noise didn't continue so she thought maybe it was her brother. She quietly walked to the area she heard the noise. As she crept up, she started getting scared: "Chris?" she whispered.

Then out jumped Chris from behind a tree: "BOO!" he shouted, "Now I'm gonna get to the 'home free' tree," he said, "catch me if you can."

Chris bolts to the area where he thinks the mītos is. Amanda screams at Chris: "Hey no fair, I'm supposed to find you first."

"You snooze, you lose!" snickered Chris, as he looked back at his sister.

Chris looked up ahead and didn't recognize the trail. Did he make a wrong turn or is he not remembering right?

He stops and calls out to his sister: "Amanda," exclaimed Chris," do you know where we are?"

"In the back yard," assured Amanda, "Our home is nearby." She said as she looked back, and front, and side by side, but everything was unfamiliar. "We're lost!" stammered Amanda.

"Hold it now," said Chris "we just need to find the mītos, and we'll be home free."

"I thought you said we'd be able to see the house." said Amanda.

"We need to be at the mītos, and then we can see the house" explained Chris.

The pair walked through an unfamiliar trail as Amanda followed closely to her brother. There were no recognizable scenes on their trek nor was there any "home free" tree or even any tree like it.

Chris was getting very worried, but he had to keep his cool for his sister, who was looking more frightened by the minute.

"What are we going to do Chris?" asked Amanda "how will we get home?"

"Stop whining like a puppy Amanda, we'll find our way" said Chris, and as he said this, he realized something "Amanda, your whining gave me an idea."

Chris started howling like a dog and startled his sister. "What are you doing?" asked Amanda, "Have you gone crazy?"

"Amanda!" shouted Chris "What nuisance is over-running the rez?" He asked.

"Dogs?" Amanda said.

"Exactly!" Said Chris, "So start howling and barking, when the dogs hear us, we'll know where to go."

"You're a genius Chris" said Amanda.

So they howled and they barked in all directions. They went on for about 10 seconds and stopped to listen. After a moment or two, they could hear dogs in the distance.

"I never thought I'd be happy to hear those darn mutts barking," said Chris.

When they got to the steps of their home, Amanda turned to her brother: "What are we gonna tell our babysitter?"

"Just relax sister" said Chris "and lets just face the music, I'm a little spent from worrying so much."

Amanda looked at Chris as if not to believe him. They walked into the house and saw the babysitter sleeping on the couch. The siblings look at each with relief. A few minutes later, their parents' car was pulling up in the driveway just as the babysitter was waking up.

"Hey kiddies, what's up" Charlene asked.

"Oh nothing" Amanda said, "we were just about to get a snack for ourselves."

The parents walked in, "Hey kids, how was your evening?"

"Good" they all answered together.

"Anything exciting happen?" The father asked.

"No, not one thing." said Chris as he winked at his sister.

Chapter Nine

Joe and the Stranger

Joe is walking down the dirt road about 20 KM from his rez. While he is tired and hungry, he has no wife or kids of his own, which means no real worries. Responsibilities are for his foolish friends, not him.

It is a beautiful night, it is more morning, about 2:45AM. The cold autumn wind and misty clouds lightly cover the moon in wisps. He has not seen a vehicle for over an hour and when he did, they were going too fast, probably a drunk driver. Good ol 'rez boys and girls, he thinks. He looks ahead further and declares, "niwī atāwakān nitahcahk simāk kita takosiniyān itī kāwīkiyān." – I will sell my soul to get home now.

At 3:00AM, about 100 metres ahead of him, there flashes a light. It was not a big light, it is more of a spark. It fades and as he gets closer, he sees another hitchhiker meeting up with him. He might be from the same rez but Joe realizes that the hiker does look familiar. When he finally meets up with him, the stranger looks all too familiar. He looks exactly like him.

"tānisi cō, tāpwī kayās." – How are you Joe, it has been a long time. Says, the stranger.

Joe stands fearful of what he is seeing. "awinōma kītha?" – Who are you?

Stranger, "cō, īmowī nihtāwikīn kāki wāpamitān, ikospi kākī nitowithihtamān kitahcahk." – Joe, I saw you before you were born, since then, I wanted your soul.

Now fearing for his soul, Joe steps ahead, "namwāc kiwī mīthitin kīkway." – I will not give you anything.

"kiwi asotamātin kīkway cō, māka kita mīthin kitahcahk" – I will offer you something Joe, but you must give me your soul.

Joe shakes his head as he takes a few steps back.

In the middle of the dark road, appears a beautiful brand-new truck, higher than two regular cars and tires as tall as Joe's chest. Joe looks in awe as the beast of an engine roars like a lion.

Joe is astonished. In all his 30 years, he never had his own vehicle, not even an "Indian" car. He drove before and loved it. If he takes the truck for the mere price of his soul, his friends will envy his masculine prowess even more. He can ride through the rez with his new sexy wheels while they dragged along their rez chicks and rez rats. He could just imagine the looks on their faces, they would be so jealous.

The stranger smiles as he anticipates the answer he craves. Men like Joe are of a rare breed of warrior. A soul, a spirit that strengthens the possessor. However, the prowess sought by Joe would be short lived, as he would surely dive into the depths of despair in short order. The wine, the drugs and fast woman would be easy to come by. Joe would be, in all his glory for the whole rez to see and then the stranger would have the full soul.

Joe explores the vehicle further; he runs his hand over the chrome bed railings. He was always the handsomest, fastest, and strongest of his friends.

However, they always had something over them, they had wheels and he did not. This truck would put him over the top. He reassured himself that a truck like this will make almost godlike, on the rez.

Joe turns to face the stranger that looks like him, and flash! He sees himself in a drunken stupor, squeezing an alcohol ravaged woman. Flash again! He sees himself fighting another native man as they stumble around like idiots, getting videoed from bystanders on their cell phones, going live on social media. Flash again! Joe sees the stranger standing and waiting for his answer.

The stranger stares at him: "tānihkōma cō?" – What is the matter, Joe? Flash again! Joe sees himself inside the crumpled truck, his body halfway out of the windshield: Dead.

Joe stares ahead and in disbelief. Would he really go down that path? Can he trust this stranger that looks like him, to even actually follow through with his gift? Joe opens his mouth and shakily states: "namwāc!" – No!

The stranger glares at Joe, "kihtwām kawāpamatin cō." – I will see you again Joe. Poof, he disappears.

Chapter Ten

Maci-Pimithākan – UFO

Mary's heart is pounding, racing like it's going to burst. She is running to her parent's cabin where she grew up and the safest place she knows. The sight she just saw was spectacular from a distance, but as she stood at the frozen shore of the lake…

Mary proudly looks at her daughter as she finishes her first set of snowshoes. The fall weather was a time of preparation for her family. The boreal forest had relentless winters that often hit the northern families hard. The family enjoyed many of the supplies from the nearest trading forts, but snowshoes were a necessity that only they themselves could count on for quality as the ones at the fort seemed to be made to sell cheaply.

Mary's daughter, Margret, felt much pride as she held up her snowshoes to her father, Daniel. Daniel pats his daughter on the head and congratulates her on a job well done. Daniel remembers all too clearly the tale his wife told him many years ago when they started their courtship.

... The lights came nearer and nearer until they were over the tips of the tall spruce trees across the lake. There the lights hovered and shimmered lightly.

A slight drop in height soon followed as they came to rest on the shore of the other side of the lake, just a thousand of her father's paces in distance.

Daniel could remember the fear and trembling as Mary told him the story of her snowshoes breaking as she ran from the machi-pimithākan (bad plane aka, UFO or flying saucer). He remembers how Mary said that nobody believed her when she got to her parent's cabin. They laughed and told her she was seeing things and only her grandmother didn't laugh, as if she understood what Mary had seen.

Mary ran as fast as her old snowshoes could take her. Soon, the frame starts to crack, she horridly recalls her hesitation to make herself new snowshoes for the winter because she wanted more time to play. She falls and twists her ankle as she quickly, regrettably, looks back at the craft that has landed across the lake. She hobbles slowly to the door of the cabin and bursts in to find her family staring at her frightened face. "machi-pimithākan!" She screams, as her family is rendered speechless by the word. Daniel recalls Mary's family giving her the benefit of the doubt and rush out to take a look.

Mary lays by her grandmother as she softly cries in horror and pain. Her grandmother tries to comfort her and reassure her that they won't come back anytime soon. Mary vividly remembers her grandmother telling her that she had seen something similar when she was a little girl. Her grandmother tells her that it is a group of spirits coming down to check on the most special of the family, a light for each previous generation that is signaling hope that the great circle will go on forever. It is a passing of the torch to the new bearer and that it is her turn. Mary wakes up still laying in her grandmother's arms. The family had gone to check and saw only a slight crevice of melted snow where they think Mary used a lit torch to melt the snow to prank them.

The family had heard stories before from grandma, but they never took it seriously. They were Christianized and were told that superstitions such as their legends were just stories and that it was an abomination to practice traditional teachings. The term "machi-pimithākan" came from recent sightings in the stories from magazines and is a translational of "evil flying device", "bad or evil airplanes" or UFO.

Mary never really recovered from the situation and felt that if her snowshoes had held out for the run, she would have gotten to the cabin on time to prove her story, but she was too late. Her regret lay with her hesitation to make new snowshoes, how lazy and stupid was she?

Mary's grandmother told her of their past when all the people were still Indians. There were no such words as machi-pimithākan or any other white man words in use at the time. It was not until the white man decided to Christianize the Indians that the old ways started to become frowned upon and even made illegal by the government. She was told not to pass on her knowledge as to discourage the Indian-ness of her people.

The spirits of the past have always come to visit in each generation when the torch bearer would tell the tale of hope that we were all part of the circle. A signal that the current bearer would pass and go with the spirits back to the next world and the new bearer would keep the promise of hope.

As Mary listened to the laughs and the harsh scolding, she turned to her grandmother who had fallen asleep. She gives her an ever-gentle push as she moves her face close to hers but instead, her grandmother gently falls limp on her back. Tears fall down Mary's face as she realizes what happened.

Daniel recalls Mary telling him that she tried telling the family what really happened that it was the spirits that were visiting, and she might be the new bearer. They all just laughed until they realize too that grandma was no longer with them, Mary knew her precious grandmother had gone to join their ancestors in the never-ending circle of life.

Chapter Eleven

The Eagle Flies into the Past

One day, an eagle had returned to the north on the month of his name, mikisiw pīsim, March. He was happy to be back and greeted many of his friends, "tānisi mōswa, mīna kihtwām kiwāpamatin" – "How are you doing moose, I have seen you again."

mōswa responded, "namwāc nānitaw, mikisiw, ninanāskimon ī-wāpamitām kihtwām." – "I am fine eagle; I am thankful to see you again."

Mikisiw, flew over a pack of wolves, "tānisi mahikanak, nimithīthihtīn ī-wāpamitakwāw." – "How are you wolves doing, I am happy to see you again."

"namwāc nānitaw, mikisiw, kitakahkinākosin." – "We are fine, eagle, you look great," the wolves responded in unison, as they admire the great bald eagle.

The eagle flew over his territory to begin a day's hunt for a scarce meal. He flies over treetops and over raging rivers. If it was not for the nearby human towns, the landscape would be so beautiful, he can only imagine what it used to look like.

How the land and waters must have looked in days past. However, garbage and smog are the reality he lives in. In the distance, he sees a floating circle of leafless trees, twirling in a counterclockwise motion. He had never seen such a phenomenon in his life.

He flies closer to the circle as he wonders what it could be. As he looks through to the other side, he sees the same landscape without the smog he has grown accustomed to. mōswa calls out to him, "kāwitha ikotī isi pimithā, namwāc kikiskīthihtīn kīkway anima katihtipathik." – "Do not fly in that direction, you do not know what that is, that is rotating."

mikisiw, ignores mōswa and flies even closer because he sees something wonderful. He makes one last turn and flies into the circle of wonder. Suddenly, he gets sucked into the leafless circle and tumbles through the air and falls to the ground. He collects himself and gets up. He looks up to the circle, only to see it collapse into itself.

mikisiw, jumps into flight and makes his way to the river. Only this time, there is an increased flow of fish than just 10 minutes before. Where did they come from? Earlier, there were barely more than a few fish when he flew over to greet mōswa.

mikisiw explores the vast area which is his territory. He is in awe of the pristine beauty of it all. Did he die and go to the next world? Is this place where his ancestors go to when they pass? He has no idea, but he enjoys the air and the great meals he can have in this world.

A bear near the river looks up at mikisiw, "awina ōma kītha?" – "Who are you?"

"mikisiw, nitisithīhkāson, kītha māka?" – "My name is mikisiw, what about you?"

"maskwa nitisithīhkāson,"- "My name is maskwa" replies the bear.

mikisiw flies away to explore some more. It is a new world and a chance for a new beginning. As a young eagle about to find a mate, he is happy it will be at such a beautiful, untouched place. He sees a nearby tree branch he can sleep on and get ready for the next day. As he is about to land, a rush of air sucks him toward the sky. He knows what it is: "TĀNIHKI?" – "WHY?" He screams as he is rolling rapidly into the circular, leafless twigs.

When eagle wakes up, he is laying on a pile of garbage on the side of a dirt road. This is his reality and the reality of our mother earth. It was not him, mōswa, maskwa or any other pisiskiw (animal), it was the humans who did this.

Today, almost all humans are doing this.

kfyukf

Chapter Twelve

Sōniyāw Reserve

It is another Christmas season for the community of Sōniyāw Reserve. John works in his trading post regardless of the season and always thought Christmas was a waste of money, especially when people should be buying food. It was bad enough people spent their money on alcohol and bingo but why waste it buying gifts for other people when they could be buying things for themselves.

His only employee, George, while usually quiet at his desk, is humming Christmas carols as he types on his ancient computer, punching in the inventory with every item humming as he clicked. John starts to tire of the noise, but he decided to let it slide this time. George does not seem himself, but the season has a way of doing that to people.

George stands at the door before he leaves and nervously looks at John, John notices this, "What is it George?" John grumps, knowing it will be about the wretched day tomorrow.

"Um John, I was wondering if I could leave early tomorrow," George asks, looking at the floor, "it's a special day for my family and Jimmy is happy to see another Christmas with us his family."

John palms his face, "George, the inventory is not going to do itself, there are more furs than usually because of the stupid day tomorrow and I need it done."

"I can be back later tomorrow to finish a half days work," George pleads, "I really want to be there for my family as soon as I can and I can leave enough firewood for the afternoon tomorrow so you won't have to hire another person to do it."

John in all his wisdom of not getting heat installed in his old lodge becomes interested, "You will do my wood for the afternoon tomorrow? Are you expecting extra pay or something because it ain't happening you know?"

"Of course, not John, no extra pay, consider it a gift from my family."

"As a gift? No don't be ridiculous, I have the gift of money and independence I don't need a gift." John grumbles as he looks away in disgust and pride. "Trust me, if I ever NEED anything, it won't be from anybody in this pathetic place." He continued, "Just never mind the wood tomorrow and come in tonight to finish your work that you're getting paid for and don't try to claim overtime because that is not happening either."

"Thank you John and have a happy holiday." George utters, "Good night."

John can't stand the greeting, "Merry Christmas" what the heck is so merry about it? Shopping around, spending, more like wasting money on gifts. The people in this community are drunk half the time and spend what they have left to "house BINGO" what a joke they turned out to be.

Back in the day his boss was the same way, buying gifts, giving discounts and adding candies to the supplies people would buy and the old inventory used to include gift ideas, with a discount of course. The folks here loved his old dead boss but as far as he was concerned, he was only enabling the losers and saving them money to squander on booze and bingo. "Oh Andrew," John starts, "you were such a fool, where did it get you eh? 6 feet underground and nothing to show for it, you sold me the business and you died with many of your fair-weather friends gathering around you. Poor buggers were only crying for the gravy-train you were, nothing more."

Just as John starts to walk to his den, there is a knock at the door: "Who in the blazes is that?" John mutters.

He opens the door to see two rough looking winos that may have seen better days. It was hard to say if they were this way from birth or were made this way by making idiotic decisions. John decides to humour them: "What the heck do you want?"

"Good evening, John," one starts, "can you help a couple of ol' classmates, ha ha, we want to know if you can spare a bit of food."

John barely contains himself, he wants to bash the wino's face in but he relents, "Listen you bum, I don't want you or your fellow loser coming around here to ask for food or change or whatever else you can't earn for yourself. I am sick and tired of you helpless-by-choice maggots trying to get sympathy from me, now get the heck off my property!"

"Band property," One corrects him.

"JUST GET OUT OF HERE!" John is steaming at this point as he drives off the poor homeless men before him.

The two men scurry off to the reserve street where they almost stumble and fall. John stares at the men with an icy look that would turn anything warm and cozy into a block of ice. The appearance of John's face is one of satisfaction as the men bumble about like the idiots, he thinks they are. His stare turns icy again as he sees his neighbor from across the street taking the men into their warm and toasty home. He thinks the visit is for the night: "Fools!" He yells out, but the neighbors, who know him well, don't pay attention and shut their door with a defying thud.

John believes people could not be any stupider or more foolish with their so-called acts of kindness. It is his belief that people only help others to look good in front of their peers as to appear good and kind. He never really cared what other people thought because their opinion was never any good anyway. There was only one person he wanted to impress, his old partner from way back, Thomas.

Thomas has since passed away but he died a happy fellow that still had much in the way of money and an inventory so vast as to leave John with much, much assets. The funeral was sparse in attendance but the legacy the man left behind was much more important than the presence of a bunch of freeloaders.

John stands at his back window to take in all beauty his trading post has provided for him. At the edge of the yard that holds his bow target, he notices a man standing with only his pajamas on. "Another bum." he says to himself as he searches for his glasses to get a better look but when he finds them and puts them on, nobody is in sight. "Good riddance." He mutters.

John wakes to the sound of chains dragging on the floor in the hallway. He thinks that maybe a mouse is dragging a mouse trap with him from one of the cracks on the wall. He hears it again but this time it sounded more like leg-hold traps his old partner used to use to mangle animals' limbs before they died.

He hears the door creaking as he peeks over his blanket, "who's there?" He says, just above a whisper, "I have a gun beside me." He continues.

"John-John, you would not hurt an old friend, would you?"

John uncovers the rest of his face to get a look at the intruder, and there he was, Thomas, the only one who ever called him John-John. "Thomas?" John stammers, "It can't be, your dead, you died a long time ago."

"Yes, I did," Thomas answers, "it has been a long time and I have only suffered."

"Thomas, you were the best, the best businessman I have ever known. You and I did so much for the community, why would you be suffering?"

"We didn't share John, our culture is plainly clear on that, we need to share, and the rewards are the happiness of our people."

"The people?" asks John, "The people are nothing but a bunch of spoon-fed idiots who needed our supplies, our inventory was always one of abundance. Without us, the people would have nothing."

"Yet here I am, forever bound to drag every trap and snare for every animal I could have shared and given, instead I would save the meat for myself or throw it away instead of having to "contribute to freeloaders" as we would say."

"Just take them off, don't be an idiot, Thomas!"

"There is a more dreadful fate awaiting you, John." Thomas warned, "a fate so terrible that the journey in the circle of life would take an eternity."

"Circle of life?" John asks, "Are you on the journey?"

"I needed to stop and warn you, you need to change John, before it's too late."

"I see no need to change, I am doing so well John, I have everything and so do you."

"What do I have but the fate I have given myself. The suffering is real John, constant pain, constant reminders that it could have been different, you can change John."

"I don't want to change, I won't change, you have gotten too soft Thomas, pick yourself up, you only…"

"ENOUGH!" Demands Thomas: "There will be three others to come after me to warn you. I just wanted to stop, to tell you it is not too late now, but now is the time."

John looks away from his friend, "Get out of here! Leave me alone, I don't need to do anything." John looks up and sees an empty space. He wakes up to find himself exactly the way he was when he fell asleep. "Thank goodness," he declares, "it was only a dream." John goes back to bed and falls asleep.

John wakes up to see a large eagle standing right beside his bed. The sharp beak and piercing eyes command a fear that few have ever had to endure. John looks blankly at the commanding presence and barely can utter a word, "wha…"

"I am the Eagle, spirit of Giving past," says the entity as she looks a down at the petrified man lying before him, "in the past our people had the strength and the pride of an eagle, proud as the caregivers of their nests and their young."

John finally finds his voice, yet quietly, "What do you want?"

"I am here to remind you of your past."

Suddenly John finds himself at a foggy meadow standing beside the Eagle. He looks off to his right to see an elderly fella skinning the hide of a deer, it is his father, long since departed of this earth. His father stands there talking to somebody else, it is John when he was younger.

"John, please do as I told you to do."

"Dad why do we have to give out my deer, I'm the one who killed it."

"John, we have to share what we kill to those in need, we will have plenty left over for ourselves."

"People in need should go out and kill their own deer, we don't need their handouts."

"John, it is not a handout or charity, it is the way we do things in our culture."

"Nobody cares about our culture, drinking and bingo are not our culture."

"That is true but social gatherings and giving is important, people just have different ways of doing those kinds of things even if it's not in their best interest."

"They can get their own is all I'm saying."

The Eagle looks at Johns expression and sees little difference. "John, this is the point where you should have learned your values, but you insisted on going your own way." The Eagle points to a young couple living in a shack, the young man goes outside to wait to get picked up for work, but it doesn't happen. The young mother and her baby have little to eat, and it looks like there won't be anything to improve their situation anytime soon.

"So what if their hungry, the young man should go out hunting not mopping around doing nothing, besides there has to be someone who can spare some food."

"He has been waiting to go to work, their families live in overcrowded houses and their trap-lines are depleted and are being shared by their older siblings who are also just trying to survive."

The baby starts to cry in the arms of his parents as his hunger increases. "These are the people in need that your father wanted to share with but YOU John, wanted to keep the meat to yourself."

"Get me out of here, I don't want to see poor people crying, get me home right now," screams John as he turns around to find himself in his living room downstairs. "How did I get here?" He asks himself.

As he turns to go upstairs, he bumps into a moose man standing there with his antlers wide and strong but with a calmness he can feel. "Oh no, not another one," John says as he palms his face, "who are you now?"

The moose man looks at John with sad suffering eyes, "John, I am Moose, spirit of Giving present, not a predator but a survivor among predators."

Moose and John are standing outside the window of his employee's run-down house. George is bringing a big bowl of fried potatoes to the centre of the table. "Dad, what is for supper?"

"FRIED POTATOES!" shouts George, with over done jubilation.

"YAY!" Jimmy yells, "potatoes again."

John is flabbergasted, "What is so good about a big ol' bowl of potatoes?"

"They are being sarcastic," Moose explains, "this is probably the fifth night they've had to eat potatoes for supper."

"That's not too bad, as long as they're eating something, that's good, way to go George just like a man should be."

"With the meager salary you pay him, he can't afford more than what they have."

"Well kudos to ol' George, he has done well for himself."

Six-year-old Jimmy turns to his father, "Dad, maybe these potatoes are making me worse, the pain seems worse after I eat them."

"When I can save more money, we can send you off to a specialist, but this is all I can do for now. Sally dear, come to the table with us." George says as he gathers his loving family and hold hands, "I would like to give thanks for the meal we are about to receive and blessings to all mankind." George continues, "and I would also like to thank my employer John for his trust in me."

"Ha!" Sally says, "why do you even mention that decrepit old man, he could have at least gave you a bit of a Christmas bonus."

"Sally, John is alone tonight, his family is all but gone with only distant siblings who are like him."

"Cheap?"

"No dear, they like to keep to themselves." George declares as he notices Jimmy bending over in pain, he runs to his side, "Jimmy, oh my poor boy, just hold for a few seconds, it will go away."

John looks away, "Please take me back."

The Moose can sense the guilt in Johns words, "Why John? Do you actually care?"

"Of course, I care you stupid Moose now let us go home, I grow weary of your mind games."

John wakes up in a heaving sweat. He quickly looks around for the moose man and reassures himself that it was just another nightmare. He walks over to his den to look at some paperwork that George will need to work on the next day. He carefully looks over some data and sees movement at the corner of his eye, at the wind frosted window facing one of the trees in his massive yard. He shrugs it off and continues his work. Again, he sees something but he does look directly this time hoping it will just go away. The movement seems to increase. This time he looks up to see a great horned owl the size of a man deathly staring at him. Johns jumps up off the chair, "Cheese and crackers, what now!" He yells.

The Owl, spirit of Giving future, a symbol of death in Indian culture, does not make a sound. He only stares as if to know what John is thinking. He points to a place where there is no love for man in the winter, the street. John and Owl stand at a street corner as a couple hold each other as they cry walking to their empty humble house, "There was nothing that could be done Sally dear," George says as he tries to assure his wife that things just happen sometimes for odd reasons.

"If we had the medicine, he would still be with us."

"Darling, we still have each other but you are right, there was just no money."

"Just no money, John could have paid you what you deserve, and Jimmy would still be with us."

John looks on in shear guilt, "No not Jimmy, the poor boy." Owl just stands there and makes no motions or even stirs a bit. "You did this didn't you Owl? You are the death symbol therefore you could have done something, it's all on you. If not you then who?"

Owl brings up a huge dark wing over John and brings it down to reveal a new sight. Two men are carrying shovels as they walk away from the local graveyard. They are talking about somebody. "Well, that was quick, just a burial and no real funeral." Says one of them.

"Tell me about it, he has the most expensive plot and tombstone but nobody there to bid him farewell, ha ha, another classmate bites the dust. What did we do to live so long?"

"Good genes and good jeans, they keep the body from falling apart."

"This old man only wore the finest even to his grave, after I spit on it, I dug up some nice cufflinks."

The other man starts laughing, "Hahaha, all dressed up and nobody shows up."

"Hahahaha, poor bugger"

John feels outright sympathy for the recently deceased, "Who is this poor soul that nobody attends the funeral?"

Owl leads John to the lone grave and points at the tombstone with his large wing. John bends to get a good look, he can barely make out the name in the dark but then he sees it, JOHN

John takes a stumbling step back, "No, no it can't be, this can't be, you have to do something, I can change, Jimmy doesn't have to die, I can't die like this, I'll change," John cries, " I promise I'll change, I can take care of everything, I'll change, " John goes on his knees, "I'll change, I'll change, I'll chan..." Suddenly, he is in his living room floor. "What? Where am I?" John gets up and peers out the window. "there's still time, yes, there's still time." He opens the window and shouts out "I'm home, I'm back!" There is a soft knock at the door, more of a gentle rapping.

John opens it to find the same two men that came by yesterday, "Merry Christmas gentlemen, welcome, come on in."

The two men look behind themselves to see who John is talking to, "This our last plea for food, please, we are hungry."

"Hungry?" John yells, "no need to be hungry, here hang on." John runs to his fridge and pulls out a rack of ribs, "Here take my best ribs, and here take my bread, cheese and whatever else."

"Thank you," says one thankfully, "are you alright sir?"

"Never been better, you boys need a ride somewhere? Here take my snow machine keys, drive around and live a little, here's some money buy yourselves something."

"Thank you, sir, ol' classmate, if you are our ol' classmate." Questions the other man.

"Yes, old classmates, now run along I have things to do today."

The men jump on the snow machine and drive off. John looks around his home with a new sense of life. He skips over to his den and there he finds the data on inventory and his finances, "From now on, things are going to be different.".

About the Author

As a child, I went to trapline many times with my parents and siblings. Much of my time was spent with my late grandfather. He taught me to tell stories with hand gestures and facial expressions that help to visualize the events as they are happening. I use Cree words as best as I can, however, many stories were written before my writing skills improved through education.

When we were not in the trapline, I would be on the reserve with my maternal grandparents. They had a TV, and a collection of encyclopedias and National Geographic magazines, that I devoured when I was not playing outside and exploring the surrounding area.

About The Publisher

O'MAHK'SIIK'IIMI (aka Jason EagleSpeaker)

Only a few short years after the Occupation of Alcatraz, the Wounded Knee Incident and the Shootout at Pine Ridge Reservation, a boy was conceived. Born in Seattle, raised on four reservations and in two cities, Jason EagleSpeaker is both Blackfoot (mom) and Duwamish (dad). He is an award winning internationally published Author, Illustrator and Publisher of over 350 books (with Authors from over 300 First Nations).

His hard hitting true stories focus on revealing Indigenous peoples' modern experiences.

You can easily connect with Jason online through social media (Facebook, LinkedIn) or via his website - eaglespeaker.com

More From Eaglespeaker Publishing

NAPI CHILDREN'S BOOKS:

Napi and the Rock

Napi and the Bullberries

Napi and the Wolves

Napi and the BuMalo

Napi and the Chickadees

Napi and the Coyote

Napi and the Elk

Napi and the Gophers

Napi and the :ice

Napi and the Prairie Chickens

NapiT Uhe Anthology

GRAPHIC NOVELS:

UNeducation: A Residential School Graphic Novel

Napi the Trixster: A Blackfoot Graphic Novel

UNeducation, Vol 2: The Side of Society You Don't See On TV

LEARN SOME BLACKFOOT:

My First Blackfoot Word Book

My First Blackfoot Word Coloring Book

COLLABORATIONS:

Young Water Protectors

Young Native Activist

Sober Indian...

Indigenous Peoples for BlackLivesMatter

I Am The Opioid Crisis

The Great Cheyenne

The Empowerment of Eahwahewi

Descendants of Warriors

Hello, Fruit Basket

How The Earth Was Created

I Am The Opioid Crisis

My Ribbon Skirts

My Kokum Scarves

Crow Brings Daylight

Spite No.1 and No.2

Aahksoyo'p Nootski Cookbook

Indigenous, I Am

... and many many more at eaglespeaker.com

If you loved this book, be sure to find it Amazon and leave a quick review. Your words help more than you realize. Also, be sure to check out plenty more authentically Indigenous publications at eaglespeaker.com

Manufactured by Amazon.ca
Acheson, AB